KU-022-801

Contents

BORDER
COLLIE

AN OWNER'S
GUIDE

Carol Price

Writer and canine behaviourist Carol Price has owned, trained and bred Border Collies for over 15 years. She is a member of The UK Registry of Canine Behaviourists, specializing particularly in Border Collies and rescue dogs, and the author of the best-selling books Understanding the Border Collie and Understanding the Rescue Dog. She has written extensively for *The Times* on canine and other animal behaviour subjects, and is a regular contributor and training/behaviour advisor for both of the UK's top-selling dog magazines, *Dogs Today* and *Your Dog*. Carol is currently the devoted owner of three Border Collies – Ilona, Arun and Lara – who are mother, son and daughter respectively.

David Taylor B.V.M.S., F.R.C.V.S., F.Z.S.

David Taylor is a veterinary surgeon and author who has worked with a wide spectrum of animal species for many years. Founder of the International Zoo Veterinary Group, he has had patients ranging from the King of Spain's Giant Pandas to gorillas in West Africa and killer whales with frostbite in Iceland. He has written over 100 books on animal matters including many best-selling dog books and seven volumes of autobiography. The latter formed the basis for three series of the BBC television drama *One by One*. He lives in Hertfordshire, England.

BORDER
COLLIE

AN OWNER'S
GUIDE

CAROL PRICE
HEALTHCARE BY
DAVID TAYLOR

Collins

First published in 2009 by
Collins, an imprint of
HarperCollins*Publishers*
77-85 Fulham Palace Road
Hammersmith, London W6 8JB

www.harpercollins.co.uk

Collins is a registered trademark of HarperCollins Publishers Limited

This edition published in 2011

15 14 13 12 11
10 9 8 7 6 5 4 3 2 1

© HarperCollins*Publishers*, 2009

A catalogue record of this book is available from the British Library.

Created by: SP Creative Design
Editor: Heather Thomas
Designers: Rolando Ugolini
Photography: All photography by Richard Palmer and Rolando Ugolini with the exception of
the following: page 74 *Your Dog* Magazine; and pages 25, 33 (bottom), 50 and 95 Carol Price,

ISBN: 978-0-00-743668-2

Printed and bound by Printing Express Ltd, Hong Kong

Acknowledgements
The Breed Standard on pages 18-19 is reproduced by kind permission of the Kennel Club.
The publishers would like to thank the following for their help in producing this book:
Chris Gardner and Zack, Jill Matthews with Skye, Murphy and Chudleigh, Jan and Danielle
Hall and Meg, and Anna and Ian Johnson for the use of Ella. Also thanks to Angela Gillespie,
Kathy Frawley, Josephine and Glyn Evans, Kay Randall, Lisa Holmes and Angela Robinson.

Author's acknowledgements
I would like to thanks the following for their help: Toni Jackson (Elbereth Border Collies)
and Judita Preiss (Anadune Border Collies), whom I have always found to be a mine of
information. And finally… my own three beloved dogs – Ilona, Arun and Lara. Thanks for
your patience, loyalty, willingness and kindness, and for always believing in me and giving
me your best. I cannot believe my luck in owning dogs like you.

Note: Dogs are referred to as 'he' throughout to avoid 'he'/'she' each time or the rather
impersonal 'it'. This reflects no bias towards males, and both sexes are equally valuable
and easy to train.

PART ONE

YOU AND YOUR DOG

Border Collies are becoming increasingly popular pets and companion dogs for people who see this traditional working breed as 'having it all' – namely, good looks, intelligence, high trainability and exceptional athletic prowess. Owning a dog is a huge responsibility but extremely rewarding. When you welcome a Border Collie into your home, you have to consider that he will need exercise, feeding, games and companionship as well as daily care.

Chapter 1

History of the breed

From being a dog that, barely three or four decades ago, was rarely seen beyond a farmyard, and which was bred almost solely for the purpose of working livestock over vast distances, and often highly challenging terrain, the Border Collie has since proved itself capable of not only adjusting to a multitude of different roles and pursuits but also excelling at them. Obedience, Agility and Flyball competitions, Working Trials and even Heelwork to Music events – the modern Border Collie now dominates them all, as well as winning honours in the show ring and displaying a talent for Search and Rescue and sniffer dog work.

Working roots

Over and above all these new activities, however, Border Collies, at their genetic heart, still remain, first and foremost, sheepdogs. They have been genetically programmed for centuries to possess a high level of energy and a range of instincts and sensitivities which are consistent with their earliest working role. However, these can be a problem for owners who do not sufficiently understand or correctly handle them.

The Border Collie's history as a breed is generally thought to date back to the droving or general stock dogs used by Celtic tribes in Ireland and Scotland around 2,000 years ago. It is also believed that the word 'Collie' is an adaptation of the Celtic word for 'useful'– and that Border was later added to the breed's name due to the border country between Scotland and England where these dogs traditionally worked.

Over time, it is likely that these original 'Collies' were interbred with even more exceptional livestock working dogs brought over by the Romans when they invaded Britain. The Romans' skill appears to have lain in selectively breeding dogs that could control and manage animals – most commonly, sheep – under the command of a human master, without threatening them, which was a major genetic achievement in itself. They are also thought to have been responsible for developing dogs with a classic way of

Opposite: This happy family group shows the author and her three Border Collies, whom she has bred herself with their mother, Ilona, standing in the foreground.

stalking, 'eyeing' and herding livestock, with a mesmerising glare, which you will still see in Border Collies today.

The whole Border Collie method of working livestock is actually an adaptation of the wolf's hunting sequence, with any more predatory impulses contained through the use of skilful breeding and training.

Breed recognition

For many centuries, farmers, shepherds and their trusty Collie dogs went about their daily work with little in the way of wider public recognition – until, that is, the introduction of the first Sheep Dog Trials in Britain in 1873. At such events the skills of different sheepdogs could be displayed and compared. Then, in 1907,

the International Sheep Dog Society was formed, keeping an official record for the first time of all the top working sheepdogs and their genetic lines. It is from these top working ISDS dogs, all those years back, that our modern pedigree Border Collies descend.

It was not until 1976 that the UK Kennel Club recognized Border Collies as a pedigree breed for 'showing' purposes, which led to the drawing up of the official KC Border Collie 'Breed Standard' (see page 14) and the development of dogs with a somewhat more uniform and refined appearance, in order to better meet the demands of this standard in the show ring.

This young Collie displays classic 'working instinct' in 'eyeing' and stalking behaviour.

Appearance

Border Collies today can come in many different colours, including red, blue or sable and white, blue or red merle, and tricolour (black, tan and white) but the commonest colour for the breed remains black and white.

The Border Collie's coat is usually smooth or moderately long, and comprises a dense woolly undercoat topped with a longer topcoat for both insulation and weatherproofing. This is vital for a dog that is designed to work outside for long hours in all weathers. The Border Collie's ears can be either pricked (or erect) or tip and fold over at the top (semi-erect), although some dogs can feature one of each!

Show dogs versus working dogs

As previously highlighted, the demands of the Kennel Club Breed Standard has led to many Border Collies today, which are bred from show lines or by show breeders, developing a much more uniform size and look than those that are bred purely from working lines, where a dog's performance, as opposed to his appearance, tends to be much more of a genetic priority.

As with all breed standards, no two people may ever agree as to what exactly forms the blueprint for an ideal Border Collie, but the guidelines that have been drawn up by the Kennel Club aim to define the qualities that are essential for a dog that is designed to work tirelessly and athletically, move well, emanate intelligence and be pleasing to the eye.

BORDER COLLIE COLOURS

The commonest coat colours are: black and white; black, tan and white (or tricolour); and red and white, although there are many other 'merle' or 'diluted' colour variations available.

Growing popularity

It is often thought that the televizing of sheepdog trials – most notably the BBC's *One Man* and *His Dog* series – from the 1970s onwards, was greatly responsible for the massive subsequent increase in the Border Collie's appeal for pet owners. Such growing popularity, however, has not come without a downside, as people with less experience or knowledge of this highly driven working breed have often struggled to understand its somewhat unique psychology and instincts, or found themselves unable to meet its more demanding mental and physical needs. Other people simply got their dogs from less appropriate sources, as

Border Collies are versatile dogs who need to be occupied and thrive on the companionship of their owners.

outlined in the next chapter. The end result, sadly, has been a flood of Border Collies entering behaviourists' clinics and rescue centres in recent years, and the dog, unfairly, acquiring a reputation as a 'problem pet'.

Border Collies are dogs who love outings and adventures and being involved in everything that happens within their family 'pack'.

Rewarding companions

When correctly bred, reared, socialized, trained and handled, the Border Collie can be the most exceptionally rewarding of companions. This is an incredibly loyal, versatile, willing and intelligent dog, with not only a sense of humour but also a generous heart. It is not a dog who will suffer fools gladly, but at the same time its inherent sensitivity means that it can react very badly to any forms of harsh or insensitive handling.

The Border Collie, ultimately, has a long and noble history of working side by side with mankind over many centuries and, despite all its newer and ever-changing roles and functions, it still remains the finest sheepdog the world has ever seen.

If you respect your Border Collie, its essential character, genetic legacy and daily needs, then he will respect you in return, and you will find yourself with a rewarding and intelligent canine companion beyond compare.

Breed Standard

General appearance Well proportioned smooth outline showing quality, gracefulness and perfect balance, combined with sufficient substance to give the impression of endurance. Any tendency towards coarseness or weediness undesirable.

Characteristics Tenacious, hard-working sheepdog, of great tractability.

Temperament Keen, alert, responsive and intelligent. Neither nervous nor aggressive.

Head and skull Skull fairly broad, occiput not pronounced. Cheeks not full or rounded. Muzzle tapering to nose, moderately short and strong. Skull and foreface approximately equal in length. Stop very distinct. Nose black, except in brown or chocolate colour when it may be brown. In blues nose should be slate colour. Nostrils well developed.

Eyes Set wide apart, oval shaped, of moderate size, brown in colour except in merles where one or both or part of one or both may be blue. Expression mild, keen, alert and intelligent.

Ears Medium size and texture, set well apart. Carried erect or semi-erect and sensitive in use.

Mouth Teeth and jaws strong with a perfect, regular and complete scissor bite, i.e. upper teeth closely overlapping lower teeth and set square to the jaws.

Neck Of good length, strong and muscular, slightly arched and broadening to shoulders.

Forequarters Front legs parallel when viewed from front, pasterns slightly sloping when viewed from the side. Bone strong but not heavy. Shoulders well laid back, elbows close to body.

Body Athletic in appearance, ribs well sprung, chest deep and rather broad, loins deep and muscular, but not tucked up. Body slightly longer than height at shoulder.

Hindquarters Broad, muscular in profile sloping gracefully to set-on of tail. Thighs long, deep and muscular with well turned stifles and strong well let down hocks. From hock to ground, hindlegs well boned and parallel when viewed from rear.

Feet Oval in shape, pads deep, strong and sound, toes arched and close together. Nails short and strong.

Tail Moderately long, the bone reaching at least to hock, set on low, well furnished and with an upward swirl towards the end, completely graceful contour and balance of dog. Tail may be raised in excitement, never carried over back.

Gait/movement Free, smooth and tireless, with minimum lift of feet, conveying impression of ability to move with great stealth and speed

Coat Two varieties: 1) Moderately long; 2) Smooth. In both, topcoat dense and medium textured, undercoat soft and dense giving good weather resistance. In moderately long-coated variety, abundant coat forms mane, breeching and brush. On face, ears, forelegs (except for feather), and hindlegs from

hock to ground, hair should be short and smooth.

Colour Variety of colours permissible. White should never predominate.

Size Ideal height: dogs 53cm (21in); bitches slightly less.

Faults Any departure from the foregoing points should be considered a fault and the seriousness with which the fault

A fine example of a male pedigree Border Collie in top condition.

should be regarded should be in exact proportion to its degree.

Note Male dogs should have two apparently normal testicles fully descended into the scrotum.

© The Kennel Club.

The Border Collie

Coat Two varieties: 1) Moderately long; 2) Smooth. In both, topcoat dense and medium textured, undercoat soft and dense giving good weather resistance. In moderately long-coated variety, abundant coat forms mane, breeching and brush.

Body Athletic in appearance, ribs well sprung, chest deep and rather broad, loins deep and muscular, but not tucked up. Body slightly longer than height at shoulder.

Tail Moderately long, the bone reaching at least to hock, set on low, well furnished and with an upward swirl towards the end, completely graceful contour and balance of dog.

Hindquarters Broad, muscular in profile sloping gracefully to set-on of tail. Thighs long, deep and muscular with well turned stifles and strong well let down hocks. From hock to ground, hindlegs well boned and parallel when viewed from rear.

Size Ideal height: dogs 53cm (21in); bitches slightly less.

Gait/movement Free, smooth and tireless, with minimum lift of feet, conveying impression of ability to move with great stealth and speed

Eyes Set wide apart, oval shaped, of moderate size, brown in colour except in merles where one or both or part of one or both may be blue. Expression mild, keen, alert and intelligent.

Ears Medium size and texture, set well apart. Carried erect or semi-erect and sensitive in use.

Head and skull Skull fairly broad, occiput not pronounced. Cheeks not full or rounded. Muzzle tapering to nose, moderately short and strong. Skull and foreface approximately equal in length. Stop very distinct.

Mouth Teeth and jaws strong with a perfect, regular and complete scissor bite, i.e. upper teeth closely overlapping lower teeth and set square to the jaws.

Neck Of good length, strong and muscular, slightly arched and broadening to shoulders.

Forequarters Front legs parallel when viewed from front, pasterns slightly sloping when viewed from the side. Bone strong but not heavy. Shoulders well laid back, elbows close to body.

Feet Oval in shape, pads deep, strong and sound, toes arched and close together. Nails short and strong.

Chapter 2

Acquiring a puppy

Getting any dog is always a massive commitment, which should only ever be undertaken by those prepared to safeguard its daily needs and overall welfare throughout its entire lifetime.

The right dog for you?

Border Collies can be more demanding than most dogs, so before you actually acquire one it is worth considering what changes you might have to make to your lifestyle and daily routine in order to own one successfully. Although they can vary tremendously in their individual character, Border Collies are an immensely energetic working breed – they don't do 'pottering'. These dogs crave set daily routines, regular mental stimulation, plenty of physical exercise – no matter what the weather – and relentless training to keep them suitably occupied and their working instincts and behaviour under optimum owner control.

If you are an active person who relishes the challenge of owning and training an incredibly smart dog, and you have a committed approach to the daily routine of caring for animals, then it is hard to think of a breed that would

suit you better than a Border Collie. If not, do not get this breed on a whim and then wonder what went wrong; it is your dog who will ultimately pay the highest price for your mistake.

Sourcing a puppy

The one thing all Border Collie puppies have in common is that they are cute, fluffy and highly appealing. However, imagining that you can get one from any source, or background, and he will still have the same capacity to make an ideal social companion or family pet, can prove to be a costly error, resulting in a more problematic, or simply a genetically inferior, dog.

Avoid disreputable sources

Many people make the mistake of buying Border Collie puppies cheaply off farms, without knowing anything about their true genetic background, in terms of both their health and temperament. Sometimes the gamble pays off and they end up with a good dog, but there's still

Opposite: Border Collie puppies always seem irresistible, but they will grow up into more demanding adult dogs.

too high a risk that the Collies they buy will have a higher incidence of genetic faults in their health or temperament, or they may just not have the kind of personality that can cope with life as a social companion or family pet.

Alternatively, they may buy them from pet shops, small ads or even middlemen who 'helpfully' offer to deliver a puppy to their door, or meet them with it at a motorway service station to 'save them a longer journey'. All these outlets and ruses are classic ones used by puppy farmers to offload their invariably inferior dogs onto an unsuspecting public purely to make money. Once cash has changed hands you will find not only that the puppy they have left you with may be sickly, nervous or temperamentally unsound, but also that they show little interest in his subsequent welfare.

Costly consequences

People sometimes say they only bought a puppy from unscrupulous sources because 'they felt sorry for it'. However, every time they do this, they simply encourage bad breeders to keep going, and inflict even more deprivation and suffering on dogs. Alternatively, they may claim that they thought they were getting a 'pedigree' dog at a bargain price. But frequently the Border Collie puppies concerned are not real pedigree dogs (see opposite) or are poorly bred ones, which may later cost their owners a fortune in vets' and behaviourists' fees – so much for a 'bargain'!

It is always worth remembering that no truly well-bred, well-reared and high-quality pedigree dog is ever sold 'on the cheap'. Sometimes distinctly inferior dogs can be hideously over-priced, so you need to look at other more vital signs and criteria, other than simple cost, when looking for your ideal Border Collie breeder.

What kind of dog?

The first thing you need to decide, before looking for the most suitable Border Collie breeder, is whether you want the dog purely as a pet, or whether you also want to show him, or compete with him in pursuits such as Obedience and Agility, as different breeders will specialize in dogs that are most suited, genetically, to these different roles or functions.

Border Collies that are bred primarily from show lines can often have more placid and laid-back natures, which makes them easier pets. At the same time, however, they can sometimes lack that extra spark of energy and brainpower, which is needed in a top working/competition dog.

In contrast, if you choose a more energetic/obsessive type of Border Collie, mainly from working lines, he may excel at Obedience or Agility, but not be so 'flashy looking' or so easy to live with as a pet. Of course, many Border Collies can be exceptions to these rules, but generally it is important to understand

how a choice of different genetic priorities by individual breeders can affect the whole look and nature of the dog you eventually own.

This red merle Collie is watching over her newborn litter of five puppies.

What is a 'pedigree'?

People often wrongly imagine that all Border Collies are pedigree dogs when, strictly speaking, they are not. Some puppies have a pure 'working' pedigree, which means that they are registered

with the International Sheep Dog Society and descend entirely from ISDS-registered stock. Other pedigree Collie puppies will be registered with the Kennel Club, on the basis that both their parents were KC registered dogs, or alternatively they may be registered with both the ISDS and the KC, which is known as 'dual-registered'.

Either way, if your puppy is sold to you as a pedigree dog, he should have the accompanying registration papers – and ISDS/KC number(s) – to prove it. In addition, you should be given a printed pedigree going back at least five generations, detailing his ancestors, from parents to great-great-great-grandparents (although you can also get these from the ISDS or the Kennel Club, once you have your puppy's relevant registration number or numbers).

If your Border Collie is not a 'pedigree' dog in the strictest sense, with the appropriate registration number and papers, then you should be charged less than for a dog with a more illustrious and officially registered pedigree line. You will not be able to show him at most Kennel Club licensed 'breed' shows, but you will be able to compete with him at KC Agility, Obedience and Working Trials events, provided that you first enter him on the Kennel Club's separate 'working register'.

This bitch has a good temperament and is content to let visitors and potential owners gently handle her new puppies.

Finding the right breeder

Once you have decided on the kind of Border Collie you want, and whether or not he needs to have a 'pedigree', your next task is to find the best possible breeder. Do not make any impulsive decisions based on purely superficial factors, such as how close a breeder lives to you, or the particular colour of the dogs they breed. Nor should you have your head turned by flashy websites or advertisements, or by the fact that a person appears on some 'recommended list' of breeders. All these things can only tell you so much when what you really need to do is to visit lots of different breeders and their establishments, in person, and just observe.

Be prepared to take your time and do plenty of research to track down the ideal breeder and puppy – it will pay off in the end. And realize that one of the most reliable tools for sniffing out any really good breeder is, in fact, your own common sense.

Using your common sense

If the very first thing any breeder tells you, abruptly, on the phone – and usually before you even ask – is how many puppies they have for sale and what price they want for them, your common sense should warn you not to even bother visiting them, as clearly they are motivated primarily by money, as opposed to quality breeding.

Similarly, if you visit an establishment that is filthy, and where there are umpteen dogs of all ages running around in squalid conditions, your common sense should tell you that just as you would not expect a superbly healthy and beautiful plant to emerge out of a background of poor nurturing and neglect, much the same applies to dogs. If this is the case, turn round immediately and go home or you could live to regret it. Many unscrupulous breeders try to overcome the barrier of potential owners' common sense by rushing them in to see their puppies as soon as they arrive. They calculate, often rightly, that once you actually see those adorable little creatures, you will forget about observing them closely and making searching enquiries and will not be able to resist buying one.

A good breeder, on the other hand, will not let you go anywhere near their puppies until they have first given you a lengthy grilling, to better establish your true suitability for one of their dogs. Do not be offended by this – see it instead as a promising early sign.

The right rearing environment

If you intend to own a Border Collie as a pet, he must have been raised as a puppy within the breeder's home, as opposed to some outhouse or barn or kennel block. I am absolutely adamant about this.

Whatever any breeder says, a Border Collie that has not spent his earliest formative weeks or months of life becoming totally at ease with all the general noises, gadgets and household appliances, social comings and goings of a typical human home is always going to struggle more to adapt to this kind of set up later in life.

What to look for

The home in question does not have to be totally spotless and pristine, but it is very important that any areas where the puppies and their mother reside are kept completely clean, and the same goes for the puppies themselves. There should be no dirty bedding, or puppies caked in stale food or faeces, or water bowls that are left empty or unclean. You need to look for signs of good basic hygiene

Newborn Border Collie puppies should look chunky, glossy, clean and content.

and a conscientious approach to the needs of both the mother and her puppies. If a breeder cannot even be bothered to maintain the most basic standards of good animal husbandry in front of visitors to whom they want to sell their puppies, it is unlikely that they have put much care into other aspects of their breeding programme, i.e. ideal genetic selection of the parents, regular worming, health screening, appropriate early training and socialization. It also makes you wonder how much worse things could be when they are not expecting some visitors!

What you want to see most of all in any Border Collie puppy rearing environment is love. You want a breeder who clearly dotes on their puppies, and cannot stop talking about them, whether discussing their pedigrees, individual personalities or health screening. Moreover, both the mother and her pups should look happy, confident and relaxed in the presence of the breeder. This is the only sort of environment I would ever want when buying a Collie puppy. You will recognize it instantly when you come across it, so keep on looking until you find it.

Assessing the mother

Much is often made of how important it is to see the puppies 'with their mother'. Undoubtedly, this can be a good way to flush out less scrupulous breeders or puppy farmers, who would prefer to present you with a cute pup in splendid isolation rather than take you to the squalid environment – usually outside their home – where it lives the rest of the time with its mother and littermates.

It is often thought that the temperament of the dam (mother) of a litter can give you some indication of how her puppies might turn out, but in reality she is only one half of the total genetic input into those dogs. What about the father (sire) of the litter and his character?

Four or five puppies are an ideal-sized litter for a Border Collie mother.

Judging temperament

When it comes to seeing a mother with her pups, be aware that giving birth can take a lot out of a bitch, both physically and psychologically. Add to this the fact that even the most mild-mannered bitch can feel a little apprehensive, or protective, about strangers handling her new babies, and you get an idea of how wrong it can be to make snap judgements about a bitch's 'normal' temperament from this kind of scenario.

It is far better to ask the breeder to let you meet the bitch well away from her puppies, once they are at least a month old, have begun being weaned, and are thus making less demands on her. Make a fuss of her, stroke her gently and see if she reciprocates in a confident, friendly way. If she does, it's likely that she is an essentially nice dog. However, if she shows any outward signs of nervousness or aggression, then beware – this would certainly be enough to put me off getting one of her puppies.

This apart, please be aware that too many breeders today (and not just of Border Collies) still blithely carry on

Like all puppies, Border Collies usually learn their vital early lessons in dog behaviour and social skills from interacting with their littermates as well as their mother.

breeding from dogs with essentially unsound temperaments, out of a belief that this fault is going to somehow stop, or go away, with the next generation. It never does, unfortunately, and sometimes it can get worse.

The father and other relatives

As mentioned above, a mother comprises only 50 per cent of the genetic input in any litter, and the father accounts for the rest, yet how often are potential owners invited to meet him, or even find out much more about him from his owner?

Instead he often remains an absent and rather shadowy figure in the background, which I find somewhat bizarre. He may have descended, reputedly, from this champion or sired that champion, or won this or that show, but what is he actually like as a dog, personality-wise? Does he have a friendly, sound temperament with no leanings towards nervousness or aggression? What health screens has he had? Ultimately, these factors should be the highest priorities for you when considering one of his offspring as a future long-term companion.

It is important to understand that a litter's pedigree, on paper, will probably mean very little to you unless you have considerable knowledge of different Border Collie blood lines, and the potential faults – as well as pluses – that might be carried in each. Thus the more you research or, ideally, meet your prospective puppy's immediate relatives on both parental sides – the father, elder brothers or sisters, aunts and uncles,

cousins and grandparents – to assess their 'typical' type of temperament and health status (e.g. any incidence of deafness, joint problems or epilepsy), the better an idea you will get of the sort of dog you should end up with.

A good breeder should help, if not actively encourage, you to do this, by putting you in touch with the appropriate owners. It may take extra time and effort to do this kind of research into your prospective puppy's overall genetic background, health and temperament-wise, but it is time well spent and could prevent you making a serious mistake over your choice of dog.

Assessing health

Border Collies can have anything from one to nine puppies, and occasionally even more, but a litter size of four to seven puppies is more normal and, indeed, more desirable. This is because there are enough puppies to interact happily and teach each other valuable canine social skills from early on, yet not too many to put undue pressure on the bitch, or to deprive some puppies of sufficient milk.

A good time to first view and assess a litter is from around a month onwards. By this age, the puppies should be able to see and hear, will be up on their feet and should have also begun the process of being weaned.

Their first baby teeth should be in position, so you can check for such faults as an imperfect bite, i.e. a jaw that is too undershot or overshot, resulting in the teeth not meeting together in a

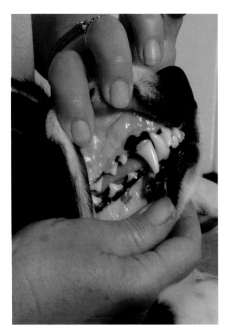

This illustrates a perfect 'scissor bite' in a Border Collie.

perfect 'scissor bite'. Be aware that puppies born with an imperfect bite do not 'grow out of it' as they get older, which you can sometimes be told. At the same time, you can check that none of the pups have a cleft palate.

A new litter of healthy Border Collie puppies should be a beautiful sight. Their coats should be wonderfully sleek and glossy, and their eyes should be bright and free of any redness or discharge. There should be no sign of diarrhoea, parasites or sickness present in the litter, and when you pick up any puppy he should wriggle energetically and feel warm, dry and chunky. His coat and ears should smell clean and sweet. A puppy's skin should be very elastic,

so if you lightly pinch it up it should instantly snap back into position. If it 'tents up' at all, this could be a sign of dehydration and potential sickness. If a puppy seems to have a pot belly but feels quite light, this kind of bloating can be a classic sign of worm infestation, as can general poor condition.

As long as the puppies seem lively, healthy, inquisitive and generally full of beans, do not worry too much if some appear a bit smaller than the others as, growth-wise, they can catch up considerably as they get older.

Assessing temperament

You will often hear it said that the 'bolder' and more outwardly confident puppies in a litter could make more challenging adult dogs, and that you should not pick a puppy that clearly seems nervous or frightened.

My own view is that a confident dog is a good one to have, and if he later becomes 'more challenging' to own, it is probably due to the way in which he has been raised, trained and handled rather than anything else.

Confidence in a puppy, however, should not involve him showing any aggression, i.e. growling or snapping as opposed to playful 'mouthing' when you are handling him or trying to remove a toy or food item. I always tend to view this as a bad sign.

If you have exceptionally nervous puppies in a litter then, more often than not, this is an indication that something has gone wrong with either their breeding or their earliest socialization with people – or sometimes both. However, many puppies can go through a distinct 'fear period' at around seven to eight weeks old – sometimes even earlier in Border Collies. They will suddenly appear far more troubled by new, or less familiar, sights, sounds, objects and experiences. This marks the onset of the development of the fear response in young dogs and is a perfectly normal stage of their development, which will soon pass if the puppy is otherwise well socialized both prior to and after this phase.

It is worth visiting any puppy that interests you several times before you acquire him, so you can better assess his true temperament rather than make snap judgements based on only one or two visits to the breeder's home.

Other considerations

Watch the puppies with their breeder. Are they interacting and playing really happily and affectionately with him or her? And is the breeder also actively encouraging you to interact with their puppies in the same way? This is a very good sign, because the breeder will be teaching those pups, from the most ideal early stage, how rewarding it is to make strong bonds with people. Border Collies who have not been taught this lesson and were left to their own devices as puppies, either alone or in the company of other dogs, will always be harder to train when they are older.

Watching how puppies interact and behave with their breeder, as well as visitors, can tell you a lot about how well they have begun relating to people.

If you have found a really good Border Collie breeder, do be aware that they will know their puppies better than anybody else, and this is why it is ultimately best for them to pick the right dog for individual owners or families, as opposed to the other way round.

Dog or bitch?

Many people will harbour personal preferences when it comes to getting a male or female puppy, which are often based on popular prejudices, i.e. bitches are easier to train, or male dogs are more likely to roam or fight, than on established fact or personal experience of owning either sex. Having owned both bitches and male dogs, my own view is that a good dog is a good dog, whatever sex it happens to be, and that most problems with dogs derive less from simple gender and more from factors such as poor breeding, training or handling.

Temperament tests

Although I have had great fun watching people perform their own 'temperament tests' on individual puppies (such as holding one down and seeing how quickly or how strongly he resists), I have yet to see a prediction done this way, or this young, that ever turned out to be truly accurate. The purpose of the tests is to predict a puppy's future adult character, but remember that dogs' characters, during earliest infancy, are

Opposite: A young Border Collie puppy begins exploring his world.

not set in stone. They still have time to keep evolving for the better, given the right owner guidance and training, as outlined in the next chapter.

When to collect your puppy

It concerns me how often I hear people say that they want to bring a puppy home from a breeder as early as possible, i.e. around six or seven weeks old, so they can 'begin' his socialization. Not only can this be a very traumatic experience for a young puppy, but it is also the earliest, and most critical, phase of his socialization, and it is better carried out by a good breeder.

Early socialization

Before any Border Collie puppy leaves the breeder, he should have been exposed, from around a month old, to all the following on a daily basis:
- New visitors of all ages and different sexes
- Being carried (until he has finished his vaccination programme) for trips into the outside world to see a wealth of new sights, sounds, people, dogs and other animals
- Getting used to traffic, planes and trains
- Wearing a collar and lead
- Car travel.

If your breeder starts and maintains this vital early socialization process during your puppy's earliest weeks, then no matter whether he is eight, 12 or 14 weeks old – I prefer my puppies not to go to new homes until they are at least 10 weeks – he should be well on the way to becoming a socially confident, well-rounded dog.

At this point, you, the owner, take over and carry on the good work. If you suspect, however, that the breeder has not been relentlessly, and conscientiously, socializing him in the way described above, it could have adverse long-term effects on his future character and behaviour. This is particularly true in the case of much older puppies.

Do your homework

Before getting your puppy, you should know about different health problems that can arise in Collies and what tests, if any, have been done to screen for them. Not all of the conditions, listed in the box below, can as yet be screened for, but ideally your puppy's parents should have tested clear for all the eye conditions, and your puppy can be tested for CEA and deafness between five and seven weeks of age.

Both your puppy's parents should have good hip scores, i.e. a total of 13 or less, to minimize the chances of hip dysplasia (see page 100) in later life.

Genetic, or DNA, tests are now available for the screening of CEA and TNS in Border Collies, and new advances in this field are ongoing.

Finally, whatever tests your breeder says your puppy, or its parents, have had, do make sure that you see, and study, the paperwork to confirm them all.

Other paperwork

If you are getting a KC-registered pedigree Border Collie puppy, your

Health tests

Generally, Border Collies are a relatively healthy breed, but they can suffer from the following conditions, which are thought to have a genetic link (see page 100):

Eye/visual disorders
- Collie Eye Anomaly (CEA)
- Progressive Retinal Atrophy (PRA)
- Primary Lens Luxation (PLL)

Other disorders
- Deafness
- Epilepsy
- Hip dysplasia

Somewhat rarer conditions include Ceroid Lipofuscinosis (CL), a disease affecting the nervous system, which can be fatal, and Trapped Neutrophil Syndrome (TNS), an immune system defect. Puppies born with this rarely survive beyond eight or nine months of age.

breeder should also provide you with a five-generation pedigree and an Owner Transfer Form. This enables you to register yourself as your puppy's new owner with the Kennel Club.

Your breeder should also give you details of your puppy's future feeding and worming programme and a wealth of extra information, or advice, in a special pack, which is designed to help you both get off to the best possible start in your new life together.

Bringing your puppy home

Try to visit your puppy as much as possible before you bring him home. Then, about a week before you do so, give his breeder one of your old jumpers or T-shirts to leave where your puppy and his mother and littermates sleep. This will give him the opportunity to get more used to your scent. In addition, the scent of his family will be transferred on to your clothing. When you collect your puppy, take this home with you and leave it in his bed as an additional source of comfort.

Equipment you will need

Here is a list of things that you will need to buy before bringing your puppy home:

- A suitable-sized puppy crate, i.e. big enough for an adult dog to stand up and freely move around in. Crates are not compulsory but, if used correctly, they are preferable to baskets for Collies. They can double up as a 'refuge zone' for them to wind

These heavy ceramic food and water bowls are ideal for most dogs.

Crates are not cruel – your Border Collie will regard his crate as his own private space.

down in, which they desperately need, being such an excitable and easily over-stimulated breed. A boisterous Collie pup would knock down the average pup play pen in five seconds and mince a basket to shreds

- Comfortable fleece bedding, e.g. vet bed
- A dog gate, approx. l.7m (3ft 6in) high
- An appropriate complete food
- Food and water bowls, preferably the heavy ceramic variety, not plastic ones
- A puppy-sized collar and lead
- Puppy toys.

You can also prepare for your puppy's arrival by doing the following:

- Make sure your garden is escape-proof and free of hazards for a young puppy, e.g. enclose or wire any garden ponds, and check all the gates and fencing
- Arrange who is going to look after the puppy should you have to go out for long periods, or go on holiday.

The car journey home

Depending on the length of the car journey from the breeder to your home, your puppy may well find the sudden separation from his mother and littermates very distressing. If this is the first time he has ever been in a car, he will be even more traumatized and may shake or shiver, whine, howl or scream in anguish and distress.

Puppies in this situation often gain most comfort from being wrapped in a cosy blanket and held on someone's lap. If you do this, however, bear in mind that they do have a habit of being sick in cars, or incontinent when distressed, so

prepare yourself accordingly. If it's a very long journey home, remember to take water for your puppy, and give him plenty of toileting opportunities en route.

Final advice

- Never bring your puppy home on a day when your house is full of noise, upheaval and visitors, such as during the Christmas holiday. For a young puppy, already stressed by separation from his family and after an unfamiliar car journey, this is like entering the jaws of hell
- Be considerate, and start your puppy off in his new home in as relaxed and peaceful an atmosphere as possible until he grows more confident about his change of surroundings
- Lastly, whatever the breeder says or recommends, never get two puppies from the same litter, be they of the same sex or different sexes. They may either fall out and fight, as they get older, or bond so intensely with each other that they become a nightmare to control or train.

Hopefully, this chapter has alerted you to all the pitfalls to avoid when looking for a Border Collie, as well as giving you the help and information you need to find the best possible breeder and puppy. The next step is to ensure that you go about raising him in the right way.

Opposite: Most Collies soon learn that toys are one of the greatest joys in life.

Chapter 3

Rearing and socializing your puppy

Turning any Border Collie into an ideal companion or family pet is not just a matter of getting one who has the right original background but also raising him in the right way. To do this successfully, you must have a sufficient understanding of your dog's intrinsic personality, instincts and needs.

Border Collies can be very excitable, energetic, strong-minded and highly manipulative dogs, as might be expected from a breed that is designed to control animals often far larger than themselves through sheer force of character.

However, they are also exceptionally sensitive dogs, psychologically, and thus easily frightened or damaged by any kind of rough or harsh treatment. The ideal owner for these dogs is someone who will handle them calmly with consistent authority, and will give them plenty of outlets for their physical energy and fierce intelligence.

Early training

Teaching Border Collies, from earliest puppyhood onwards, how to cope with the vast array of different sights, sounds and experiences that exist in a typical human living environment is a vital part of good socialization. They also need to learn how to interact with different people (see page 48). Teaching your puppy basic obedience exercises, as well as how to keep his stronger chasing/ herding instincts under better control, should also be a critical part of his early education. If you get all these things right, you should end up with a loyal, willing and obedient adult dog whom you would be proud to take anywhere.

Early rules and routines

Your puppy's basic 'education' should begin the moment you bring him home. However, before you even do this, you should have decided on a specific set of house rules for your new dog, such as where he will sleep, which areas of your home you will allow him access to, and whether or not you will permit him on the furniture. Having made a decision and worked out the house rules, you must, as an entire family or household, stick to them. It is only through failing

Opposite: Well-balanced, well-behaved and socially confident adult Border Collies only emerge as a result of the work and training you put into them from earliest puppyhood onwards.

to do this, consistently, that puppies get into the habit of trying to challenge an owner's authority – or decide that they will obey one person in a household but not another.

Similarly, you must give your puppy a basic daily routine to give him a vital sense of security in his new life with you, and ensure that his toilet training is mastered as quickly as possible.

Toilet training

To toilet train your puppy rapidly and effectively you must take him outside routinely every hour, plus each of the following times:

• When he wakes up from sleep
• After a meal or a bout of exciting play
• Before he settles down for the night.

While your puppy is 'performing' outside, you can attach a verbal command to what he is doing, such as 'be clean!' Give him a treat and praise him enthusiastically every time he goes in the 'right' place. Soon you will have a dog who will 'perform' on request.

By contrast, if you notice that your puppy is about to go to the toilet inside the home – he may circle or sniff the ground before doing this – immediately rush him outside and repeat the above. Do not be rough or harsh with him – if you do so, you will frighten your puppy. And do *not* shout at him or scold him for having an 'accident' indoors – he will not understand your anger.

Simply clean up any mess calmly while he is out of the room, and resolve to be quicker next time in anticipating when he needs to 'go'.

Travelling safely

When travelling with your puppy in the car, either secure him to rear seatbelt fittings in a dog safety harness – available from pet stores – or buy a special travelling crate. If you have a puppy who tries to bark at your car windows, a travelling crate is best. Draping a sheet over the crate can not only stop such barking behaviour but it will also minimize car sickness.

Daily routine for puppies

Apart from regular, and routine, toilet opportunities, you must make sure every day that your puppy has set play times, meal times and rest periods as well as a set bedtime.

It is also vital to take your puppy out in the car somewhere twice daily. Not only will this get him accustomed to car travel but he will also have the opportunity to meet lots of new people and other dogs, and experience many unfamiliar sights and sounds in the world outside (see page 47).

Note: Puppies must always be carried everywhere new outside until they have completed their vaccination programme (see page 104).

Feeding your puppy

When they are very young, puppies will have short bouts of manic activity but will then need to sleep a lot. As they get older, however, they will need to eat and

Above: A purpose-built travelling cage is one of the safest ways to transport your puppy in a car.

Right: Young puppies need to be fed at routine daily intervals in order to grow and develop properly.

sleep less often but will use a lot more energy through daily walks and other forms of exercise.

As a rule, puppies need around four meals a day up to the age of 16 weeks, then three meals daily until they are six months old. Thereafter two meals a day are sufficient. Beyond a year old, you can feed your dog either two smaller meals or one larger meal a day, depending on what best suits him. The amount you should feed your puppy daily, according to his age, size and weight, should be marked

These young puppies are sharing a meal together. It is important to feed them good-quality nutritious food.

on the packet of any commercial brand of food you buy. If your dog's breeder has not recommended a particular brand, or specific type of diet, for you to continue feeding your puppy and you are not sure what to give him, ask your vet for advice.

Healthy eating

For any owner, there is a mind-blowing range of foods to choose from for both puppies and adult dogs. In the main, I have found that Border Collie puppies thrive best on a high-quality dry complete food (as opposed to canned food) that provides all their nutritional needs as they grow, and is totally additive/preservative-free (i.e. hypoallergenic).

This is because such additives can sometimes have an adverse effect on their behaviour – i.e. making them more 'hyper' – as well as their digestion.

You should feed your puppy on a special 'puppy formula' of such food until he is around six months old. He should then be fed a 'junior' formula until he is a year old, whereupon you can switch to an 'adult' variety. Advice regarding what amounts to feed your young dog for his age, size and activity levels should be printed on the pack.

If you want to add milk to such food, make sure that it's goats' milk, as opposed to cows' milk, which many dogs cannot tolerate well. It is inadvisable to feed a vegetarian diet while puppies are still growing. Once your dog is mature, you can be more experimental with his diet (see page 80).

Handling your puppy

Every day with your puppy, do the following to get him accustomed to being handled. By doing this daily with your puppy from when he is really young, it will become much easier to handle him when he is older, particularly when trimming his nails, or cleaning his teeth or ears.

1 Check your pup's ears. They should be clean, smell sweet and have no excessive wax, redness or discharge.

2 Check your puppy's feet for any cuts or thorns, or for stones or grass seeds between the pads.

3 Groom your puppy all over, and check his coat for signs of parasites or any new lumps or bumps.

4 Gently but firmly open your puppy's mouth, and inspect his teeth, gums and throat.

Dos & don'ts

You should be mindful of the following advice regarding chews, nutritional supplements and exercise for your puppy:

- **DO** carry your young puppy into and out of cars until he is about 10 months old, and restrict him to three shorter (i.e. 20-minute) walks daily, instead of one or two
- **DO** give him only chew bones and items that are specially designed for puppies – these are available from pet stores

- **DON'T** give a young puppy hide chews or other larger chew items, such as pigs' ears. He could choke on them
- **DON'T** feed any additional vitamin or mineral supplements, e.g. calcium, while your puppy is growing, unless specifically advised by your vet, as these could do more harm than good
- **DON'T** over-exercise your puppy while he is growing, as this could lead to later joint problems
- **DON'T** let your puppy regularly go up and down stairs, or jump in and out of the car, or off the furniture, until he is at least 10–11 months old
- **DON'T** let your puppy jump and twist in the air to catch toys until he is older

Sleeping arrangements

The issue of where a new puppy should sleep during his first nights in his new home is one many owners agonise over. To my mind, puppies should sleep in their own kennels or 'dens', with a blanket draped over the top and three surrounding sides, from day one. This ensures that your puppy gets used to the concept of spending time on his own from the earliest opportunity, and will thus be less likely to develop separation problems later in life.

However, your puppy will still be missing the comfort and warmth of his mother and littermates, so make sure you compensate for this. Wrap a hot water bottle in a blanket, and put this under him. Give him a soft toy or two to cuddle up to and make his bed as cosy as you can.

If you like, you can put your puppy's crate in your bedroom for the first night or two, until he adapts, but then you should gradually move it a little further away each night until he is finally sleeping in his own quarter.

Be aware that the longer you leave your puppy sleeping in your bedroom, and the more often you get up to fuss or soothe him when he cries or whimpers, the worse he will cope with being left on his own when he is older.

Limiting access

Often people make raising puppies far more traumatic – and destructive – than it need be, simply by allowing them access to their entire home from the moment they arrive. This, in turn, leads to them having 'accidents' on your best carpets or furniture, until they are reliably toilet trained. They may also destroy items that are precious to you, or run off with them as 'trophies' and then refuse to give them back. This highly popular puppy game will get progressively more exasperating as your dog gets older.

Other drawbacks

Free access can also result in your puppy ultimately viewing all this 'territory', together with the fixtures and furniture within it, as being just as much his as yours. And this is what can lead to more dominant-minded dogs monopolising certain beds, chairs or parts of the home, such as the front door area or top of the stairs. As they get older, they may regard these areas as exclusively theirs and then react aggressively when anyone tries to repossess them.

By not teaching your puppy from day one that it is a 'normal' part of life to spend routine periods on his own, in his own quarters, and away from you, you will increase the likelihood of him suffering 'separation anxiety' problems when he is older.

Start in a smaller territory

Therefore it is better for a Border Collie puppy to begin his new life with you in a more limited area of territory – somewhere with an easy-to -clean floor (in case of 'accidents'), with no precious

All Border Collie puppies should be positively introduced to new people of all ages and sexes from as early an age as possible.

or potentially dangerous objects lying around, and with ready access to outdoors to promote speedier toilet training. You can also install an indoor kennel, or puppy crate, with cosy bedding there.

The most obvious area for this purpose is usually the kitchen. Separate your puppy's area from the rest of your home with a dog gate. He needs to learn, from day one, that all the main home territory, and everything within it, belongs to you and other members of the household, and that being invited into this area is a 'privilege' which is permitted at certain times, provided that while he is there he abides by your rules.

Rules and banishment

Once you have established this territorial division, decide what rules or behaviour you want your young puppy to abide by when invited into 'your' main territory. These may include:

- No nipping of people or guests
- No taking or destroying 'your' possessions; he may only play with the toys or other items you give him
- No getting up on furniture
- No rushing to the front door ahead of you when visitors arrive.

Should your puppy do any of these things, immediately say 'No! Bad puppy!' in a firm, but not frightening, tone. Then quickly give him the chance to do something 'right' instead, i.e. 'Sit' or 'Lie down' (see pages 56 and 58) and instantly reward him when he complies with a game or treat. Praise him in a really excited tone of voice and say 'Yes! Good

dog!' Then let him stay in your territory.

If your puppy will not stop his 'bad' behaviour when you ask him to and change to 'good' behaviour instead – although he must understand first what you are asking him to do – immediately

Do not shout, become hostile, or say anything. Just take him back there calmly. It's a good idea to leave a length of string attached to his collar for this purpose. Do not invite him back into your territory until he is calm and well behaved again.

Teach your dog respect

This is how you teach any young dog not just respect for your authority, territory and commands, but also that less acceptable behaviour will always have negative consequences. However,

A dog gate is useful for separating areas of the house as well as keeping your dog safe when outer doors are open.

you must be relentlessly consistent when applying your rules and the immediate consequences of defying or complying with them, or your puppy's regard for your authority will diminish progressively. By contrast, the more often you make 'good' behaviour bring great rewards for your puppy, the more you will get.

Keep control of the front door

Early on, it is extremely important to keep your puppy behind a dog gate whenever people visit your home, so he never gets the idea that he can run ahead of you to the front door to greet them.

The front door area is the place where anyone 'new' enters the 'pack territory', or existing members leave it, so who controls it can have huge significance for dogs, status-wise. Make it clear that only you, or other household/family members, decide who is coming through your front door and how they will be greeted. Thereafter you may 'allow' your dog to meet them, provided that he behaves in an acceptable way. If not, he will be banished in line with all your earlier 'rules'.

Avoid confrontations

If you do not retain sufficient authority over a breed as strong-minded and intelligent as the Border Collie from day one, all those early little 'battles of will' you lost when he was small (and which you might have considered insignificant at the time) can come back to haunt you in spadeloads as he grows older and becomes more confident about defying you.

At the same time, however, it is vital to appreciate that by reacting harshly towards dogs as psychologically sensitive as Border Collies while they are young, e.g. shouting, smacking or any other kind of rough handling, you could force them to develop defensive/aggressive patterns of behaviour through fear, which they may then carry on into their adult lives. To avoid this, always discipline your puppy through calm banishment, as previously outlined, or by imposing a command such as 'Lie down and stay down' (see page 58) and do not get involved in any unnecessary hostile confrontations with him.

Nipping

Border Collies can be instinctive nippers, especially when suddenly aroused or excited – this is a natural part of their genetic 'working' behaviour. However, it must be discouraged from as early as possible if it is not to turn into a bigger problem later on.

To prevent this happening, never get into any sort of 'rough' or 'wrestling' games with puppies, which could not only trigger them to nip ever harder but also encourage them to think that this behaviour is acceptable. Puppies learn to inhibit their biting in response to the reaction this behaviour provokes in others. So any time your puppy nips someone, get them to immediately 'yelp' loudly like another puppy would, and then immediately walk away from him or put him back in his own quarters (see page 43). If you do this consistently, he should soon get the message.

Crates or indoor kennels

The purpose of puppy crates is to provide dogs with their own special 'den' of comfort and security, away from the general hurly-burly of a busy household, keep them out of danger, e.g. eating or chewing the wrong things, when they're unsupervised, aid toilet training and get them into the habit of spending periods on their own. By placing a blanket over the top so it covers three sides of the crate, and placing comfortable bedding inside, you make it even more of a cosy refuge for a puppy.

However, no puppy or dog should ever be shut in an indoor kennel for more than two to three hours maximum at a stretch, plus overnight, as prolonged confinement of this kind is utter cruelty, and, indeed, it can often lead to the dogs concerned developing severe psychological problems in later life.

Puppies explore the limits of their own status through games with littermates.

If your breeder did not rear your puppy using an indoor kennel, he should be given plenty of time to get used to one, and build up good associations with it, before you shut him in there. You can help this process by always feeding him in his kennel, or throwing toys and treats in there for him to find. Do make sure that the kennel is big enough for your puppy to happily stand up and roam around in, with a lot of his favourite toys or chew bones.

Healthcare

Your puppy will need vaccinating against a range of potentially life-threatening illnesses at around eight and twelve weeks old, although this schedule can vary from vet to vet. Either way, your vet should tell you when it is finally 'safe' to let your puppy go anywhere, on the ground, after his final injection. For more information, see page 104.

He will also need worming regularly, up until he reaches six months of age, and thereafter around once every year, depending on the existing environmental risk (see page 106). Again, consult your vet about this.

They can also inject your dog with a special identity microchip, which could prove invaluable should he ever get lost. You should additionally, however, and by law, get a proper identity tag for your dog's collar, which provides your address and other contact details.

Socialization

As we have already seen, the correct socialization of Border Collie puppies, from a very young age, is crucial, but owners can get confused about what this process entails. It is not so much about exposing young dogs to a non-stop array of strangers or new experiences as how to control what they learn from each new encounter with them.

The more everyday and matter-of-fact you make the experience of new sights and sounds, such as traffic, trains and aeroplanes, etc., and the more positive

By law, your dog should always wear a collar outside the home with an identity tag engraved with your contact details.

This puppy is learning at a young age how to take experiences, such as strangers and traffic, in his stride.

your puppy's social encounters with different people or dogs, the more socially confident he will become. He will also be less likely to react anxiously or fearfully to such things in the future.

Stage managing social encounters

For the best results, stage manage your puppy's earliest social encounters with different people and dogs very carefully. Start by introducing him, when you are out together, to people you already know; and do the same with visitors to your home. Look really enthusiastic and happy when they approach and get them to give your puppy a treat immediately. Start with familiar people, and then

move on to people of all ages and sexes, wearing stranger clothes or hats, people in wheelchairs, with prams or carrying sticks. Always end the encounter while your puppy is still in a happy and confident frame of mind.

If he looks frightened or anxious try not to reassure or soothe him in any way, as you will simply be rewarding, and thus inadvertently reinforcing, such a reaction. Instead, totally ignore his anxiety or apprehension and ask your 'new person' to do the same. Keep chatting to the person normally and eventually your puppy should become more curious before showing sufficient confidence to approach them. At this point, give the person a treat to offer to your puppy, and praise him really well. Again, always end the encounter while he is still confident.

Meeting strange dogs

Often 'group' puppy socialization classes are not very successful for Border Collies because they find the whole atmosphere – with lots of different dogs charging about noisily – too psychologically overwhelming. Another reason may be that the person in charge of the class is not consciously keeping control of what each puppy is learning from them.

It is all too easy in such cases for a shy puppy to be intimidated or frightened by a more boisterous or bullying older puppy and thereafter develop a negative view of new dogs.

For puppies like this it is always better to stage-manage all their early social encounters with other dogs yourself. Start off with really friendly, gentle dogs whom you know will play with your puppy and not frighten him. Avoid any dogs whom you think could be even remotely bullying or aggressive towards your puppy.

Only when he has had lots of positive experiences can you begin introducing him to older dogs who will put him in his place should he show 'disrespect' or 'bad manners', i.e. snap or hold him down on the ground, but never be frighteningly aggressive towards him. This should prompt your puppy to show

submission, such as rolling on to his back – a vital lesson that all puppies must learn to keep themselves out of trouble with other dogs later on in life.

As skilful early socialization can make such a difference to the future behaviour of a Border Collie, do seek expert help while your puppy is still very young if you have any doubts about whether you are doing it the right way. It will really pay dividends later on.

Border Collies who bond rewardingly with people, early on in life, through shared play, will always be easier to train later as adult dogs.

Chapter 4

Training and competitive events

Training, and working with, dogs as intrinsically bright and responsive as the Border Collie can be one of the most rewarding pastimes in life. However, do not imagine – as so many people do – that Collies will invariably be 'easy' dogs to train or adapt to your bidding. Although, in essence, they really are incredibly quick learners, they are capable of learning the 'wrong' things in life as rapidly as the 'right' ones. Therefore it is up to you to take better charge of their whole education, from earliest puppyhood onwards. This begins with teaching them vital early life skills and lessons, such as social adaptability, respecting your authority and enjoying co-operating with you before moving on to the more formal training exercises that are featured in this chapter, which, once mastered, should prove invaluable to you for the everyday control and management of your dog.

Beginning training

You can begin teaching Border Collie puppies basic obedience exercises from as young as six weeks old. Many owners make the mistake of only starting their puppies' training when they are much older. In doing so, they miss the critical phase in their dog's early development when he will be most receptive to learning and doing what they want him to. They also ensure, alas, that he spends this precious time instead merely learning the joys of doing what he wants.

Collies are one of the cleverest and most versatile dogs to train, whether as highly intelligent and rewarding companions (opposite), or as potential champions in the Show, Obedience or Agility ring (left).

Train your dog in your local park with the distractions of traffic noise and people.

Playing and learning

The best way to start training your Border Collie puppy the following set exercises is with treats and toys, and in the context of enjoyable shared play, so that he immediately makes positive and pleasurable associations with the whole training process and interacting with you.

By making yourself, and the toys, the main targets for your Collie's obsessive working focus and drive, from day one, you will prevent them being directed instead on to less appropriate targets, such as traffic, joggers, cyclists or other dogs, when he is older.

Working through distraction

Once you have taught your Border Collie puppy the joys and rewards of co-operating with you and your commands and exercises at home, you can then start working on them when you are out and about together, in places like the local park.

You should aim to progressively increase the level of distraction, e.g. other dogs, passing traffic, familiar people and strangers, that your dog has to screen out in order to respond to your training commands and exercises.

Note: If you have any difficulty holding your puppy's attention in training, put him on a lead or special training line, which is available from most pet stores.

How dogs learn

When training your dog, it is important to remember how easy it is to confuse him, or teach him the 'wrong' lesson, simply through not attaching a reward, such as a treat or toy, to the 'right' action the instant this action happens and/or (depending on the command) while it is still happening. Praise must be used in much the same way.

A classic example of mis-timing a reward, thus inadvertently reinforcing the 'wrong' lesson or behaviour, is to give your dog a toy or treat for 'sitting' or 'lying down' while he is not actually sitting or lying down, i.e. he has already moved out of position when you reward him. This simply teaches him to sit or lie down and then immediately move out of position in anticipation of a reward.

A classic example of teaching the wrong lesson. This owner (above) has asked her puppy to sit and stay but rewards him after he has moved and got up. This teaches him to move before you return to him, or properly 'release' it (see page 59) in anticipation of a reward.

Other training tips

- When training your dog, use some special toys as rewards, which he will not have access to at any other time; this will keep his motivation high
- If you are using treats, make sure they are particularly special and tasty, such as small chunks of cheese or sausage. Remember, however, that training treats should always be used as part of your dog's daily food allowance, and not on top of it. It is the principle of the reward that matters most in training, as opposed to the size of it
- Whatever commands you choose for your dog, make sure that everyone else in your household uses the same words for these in the same tone, or your dog may get confused
- The secret of good training is to do it little and often, i.e. three or four short bursts of around five minutes a day, varying the exercises each time. And always end on a good and positive note, when your dog has done something well. Do not keep pushing or repeating exercises to the point where he gets bored or demoralized
- Only ever train when you are in a happy and positive mood. Do not train when you are feeling tired, stressed, unwell or in a bad mood – you do not want your dog to develop negative associations with the whole training process.

The exercises

The exercises outlined in this chapter are those destined to give you maximum control over your dog's behaviour at all times, and also to form the basis of a generally well-mannered and well-behaved dog you could take anywhere.

Sit

'Sit' is about the most basic obedience exercise for dogs and usually forms the starting point for all other training.

1 To get your puppy to 'Sit', simply walk up to him with a treat or toy in your hand and hold it above his head.

2 As he moves backwards to better see what you are holding, he should eventually sit automatically. As he is actually in the process of sitting, sweep your arm upwards and also say 'Sit'.

3 Immediately your puppy sits and his bottom hits the ground, give him the treat, or the toy, praise him really well and have a game with him.

Note: After several repetitions, your puppy should quickly make an association between your word and action and sitting.

Training tips

- Do not push your dog's bottom into a 'sit' – be patient and wait for him to do this of his own accord before rewarding him
- Do remember to only say 'Sit' and reward your dog while he is actually sitting
- It is always a good idea to attach a physical gesture, as well as specific words, to each command you are teaching a puppy for extra clarity.

Watch me

After 'Sit', 'Watch me' is a vital exercise to teach any puppy, because until you can hold his concentration on command, you cannot really teach him much else. When he masters this new command, you can work on holding his attention, with the 'Watch me' command and upward pointing finger gesture, for up to 10 or 20 seconds before praising and rewarding him for his behaviour.

I **Get your puppy to sit. Hold a toy or treat in your hand, just in front of your face, with your forefinger pointing up.**

2 **As soon as your puppy looks at you, say 'Watch me' while he is doing so. Praise him and give him a treat.**

3 **As a reward for his good behaviour, throw the toy for your dog to chase and have a game with him.**

Training tips

- Do not shout at your puppy or get angry or impatient if he won't watch you; this will make him want to avert eye contact with you, so he is less likely to watch
- Keep repeating the words 'Watch me' in a really inviting and encouraging tone, while your puppy is watching.

Down

'Down' is a valuable exercise to teach any Border Collie, not just to keep him safe and still in one position, anywhere you happen to be, but also to instantly stop any less desirable behaviour in your dog, such as chasing (see page 88), whether at home or out. To teach your puppy to lie down on command, first put a treat or toy in your hand and ask him to sit and watch you, as outlined previously.

2 Slowly draw your hand backwards until he slips down on to the ground to try to get the toy or treat out of it.

I Lower your hand with the treat or toy in it down towards the ground, under your puppy's nose, with your forefinger pointing outward, as shown in the photograph above. As you do so, he should start to lower himself to explore your hand.

3 As soon as your puppy lies down, say the word 'Down'. Immediately give him the toy or treat and praise him.

Training tips

- Do not ever push your dog into a 'Down' position. Be patient and wait for him to go down of his own accord
- Do remember to only reward/praise your dog while he is still lying down.

Stay

'Stay' is a command traditionally attached to the 'Sit' and 'Down' commands, and is invaluable in keeping your dog still and safe in one position, for a prolonged period, until you come back to 'release' him. It should not, however, be confused with 'Wait' (see page 60).

2 As he is watching you, take a step backwards. If he stays where he is when you move, hold up your hand and say the word 'Stay'.

3 Immediately go back to your puppy and, while he is staying still, touch him on the shoulder, say 'OK', and then praise him really well and give him a treat or toy to reward him.

I To teach your puppy to 'Stay', first ask him to sit and watch you (see page 57).

Releasing your puppy

The shoulder-touching action, plus the word 'OK', has the effect of officially 'releasing' your puppy from a stay command. In other words, he learns that he should not move until you have come back to him and done and said these things.

Any time your puppy moves, instantly put him straight back on the exact spot where you originally asked him to stay. It is through not consistently doing this, or calling him to you after telling him to 'Stay', instead of always going back to your puppy to release him in a specific way (i.e. the shoulder touch and 'OK'), that puppies get confused or progressively disrespect this command. Once your puppy understands the 'Stay' command, and knows not to move until you 'release' him, you can try practising the same exercise with him in a 'Down' position.

Wait

Be aware that 'Wait' should be a distinctly different command in your puppy's mind from 'Stay'. This is because, unlike 'Stay', the 'Wait' command means that he should remain where he is until you ask him to do something else, e.g. come to you or retrieve something, as opposed to staying exactly where he is until you release him.

When your dog is older, and your training is more advanced, he should be bright enough to know the difference between the 'Stay' and 'Wait' commands simply through the different words and tones of voice you use for each of them.

Important: Notice the use of a different hand gesture to distinguish 'Wait' from 'Stay', i.e. a hand dropped down in front of your puppy's face for 'Wait' as opposed to being held up for 'Stay'.

However, until then, and especially when first teaching these different commands to your puppy, you must distinguish distinctly between the two in the following important way:

Signal to your dog to 'Wait' and give him the command, with your finger pointing down (left), while he is either sitting or lying still next to you.

Give a 'Stay' command with your hand held up (above) when your puppy is sitting or lying still in front of you.

Recall

The reason so many dogs develop a poor recall is because their owners let them off the lead, from day one, without having properly taught and conditioned them to come back on command. All they learn is what fun it is to do exactly as they like, the minute they get away from you. Many owners also do not understand the importance of making their presence rewarding enough for their dog to want to stay with, or come back to, them.

Start teaching the recall while your puppy is very young. Decide on a word, which is always said very invitingly and excitedly, e.g. 'Come', or a sound, e.g. a whistle, to represent your command. Make a habit of using your special recall command/sound just before you play a game with your puppy, take him out for a walk or feed him a meal. This will condition him to believe that if he comes quickly to you, on your command, it will always be rewarding.

2 Every so often, call his name and give your recall command sound. If he comes back to you immediately on the line when he hears this, praise him really well, give him a treat and also a great game with a toy.

3 If he does not come, reel him back to you on the line, encouragingly and excitedly, repeating your recall sound again as he comes towards you.

4 When he gets to you, praise him and send him off again. Only ever give him a treat, toy and game when he comes back to you of his own accord, and on your first command. This will keep him motivated to do it again and again.

1 Put your puppy on a training line and let him wander randomly around your home and garden or the local park.

Boosting recall

Once this recall exercise is going well at home inside the house or in the garden, try doing it daily with your puppy when you go out. Take some treats and exciting toys with you, and remember not to let him off the training line until he is well conditioned and his recall is really reliable.

Teaching the retrieve

To teach your puppy to get things and bring them back to you, i.e. the retrieve exercise, start him off on a longish training line and put some tasty treats that he enjoys in your pocket.

2 If you are lucky, he may bring the toy back to you of his own accord, and let you take it. In which case, praise him really well. Reward him with a tasty treat, and immediately give him the toy to play with. If not, proceed as shown below.

1 Throw a toy ahead of your puppy and, as he rushes off to get it, firmly say the words 'Go get it!'

3 As soon as your puppy picks the toy up in his mouth, reel him back to you on the line encouragingly.

Three phases

Remember that the retrieve is really the three following separate training sequences:
- 'Go get it!'
- 'Bring!'
- 'Give!'

These must all be taught correctly to your puppy and then put together in one complete sequence. Taught well, it conditions dogs to believe that bringing things back to you on command, and letting you hold them, will always be highly rewarding. It is also a useful exercise for preventing your dog grabbing household objects and running off with them.

4 As he comes towards you, say the word 'Bring!'. If he comes to you with the toy but will not let you take it out of his mouth, do not get into a tugging match with it, as this will simply make him hold on to the item even more determinedly. Instead, hold a tasty treat under his nose. As he lets go of the toy, say the command word 'Give!'. Let him have the treat and then immediately give him the toy as well and praise him enthusiastically for his good behaviour.

Walking on the lead

Puppies or dogs originally pull on the lead to get somewhere quicker than you are walking. Thereafter, they only persist in the habit to escape the near strangulation that is inflicted on them by their owners who are constantly trying to haul them back.

The only truly reliable – and kind – way to stop your puppy pulling on the lead when out walking is to make this activity totally unrewarding for him.

2 Start walking, adjusting the lead so that immediately your puppy oversteps this distance, it tightens. As soon as it tightens, say something like 'Uh-huh!' loudly and immediately and stop dead.

I Start by putting your puppy on a normal length lead, and decide how far ahead of you he will be allowed to walk, e.g. a body length. I always prefer dogs to walk closely by my side on the lead. Holding the lead in your right hand, make the puppy walk beside you on your left-hand side.

3 Call your puppy back to you and then make him sit next to you and wait, before walking on again.

4 Every time your puppy is walking in the 'right' position, next to you or a body length ahead, say something like 'Close'. Praise him really well and, from time to time, give him treats to further reinforce this behaviour.

Start early

Once again, this exercise is best started as early as possible with your puppy. It requires great patience and consistency of approach for the most effective and long-lasting results. Conversely, a failure to apply these things is the reason why so many owners are never able to prevent or cure their dog's lead-pulling habit.

Training tips

- In theory, you should teach your dog to walk on both the left and right sides of you on the lead, although some dogs develop a distinct preference for one side over the other. However, tradition dictates that you always 'work' your dog – be this in showing, Obedience, or anywhere else – on the left-hand side, so you should be aware of this if you have any ambitions in these directions
- Never use choke chains, which are sometimes called 'check' chains, on your Border Collie. Not only are they cruel but they can also inflict serious neck, spine and windpipe damage and, ultimately, do not stop dogs pulling
- Extending or extension leads are also not advisable as, apart from being somewhat cumbersome to handle, I have seen these inflict some serious injuries on both dogs and owners. A longer training line is preferable.

Basic manners

A key part of owning a well-behaved dog is to teach him some basic everyday 'good manners' and emotional self-control, particularly in situations where he is likely to otherwise get over-excited or frustrated. So get into the habit of asking your Border Collie to sit and wait quietly, for at least 10 seconds, before:

- Putting on his collar and lead to go for a walk
- Letting him get out of the car at the start of a walk
- Giving him his meal
- Starting a game of any kind with him
- Allowing him to greet visitors.

Note: If he will not wait quietly on command, keep relentlessly persisting with each exercise until he does wait.

Puppies must be taught young how to better control their excitement – and more boisterous behaviour – while having a lead put on before a walk.

Anti-chase training

Chasing moving objects, of any kind, can be a very strong instinct in Border Collies, as part of their natural or genetically pre-programmed working behaviour. In any Collie, the strength of this instinct, or the age at which it will first kick in, can vary considerably. However, the best way to control it is through teaching the following kind of exercises to your puppy, well before he has got into the habit of chasing the 'wrong' things, i.e. from when he is around four months old.

Note: You should use a long training line on your puppy for the next two exercises, and he should have already been taught the 'Wait', 'Down' and recall commands.

Down on the move

The 'down on the move' is an excellent and vital exercise to stop your Border Collie chasing anything or to keep him safe in potentially dangerous situations, i.e. when he is running towards a cliff or a busy road with lots of traffic.

1 When you are out, throw a toy for your puppy. As soon as he runs a short distance towards it, tell him to 'Lie down'. Always say this command in a firm, but never overly harsh or frightening, tone.

2 When your puppy complies with your command and lies down in mid chase, wait a few seconds and then let him run on to get his toy by giving him the command 'Go get it!'.

3 When he brings the toy back to you, praise him really well and have a game with the toy to reward him.

5 Walk up to him and ask him to 'Lie down'. When he does so, praise him really well, but do not let him have the toy.

Dos, don'ts and ongoing practice

Remember to always make it clear to your puppy that he can only go on and get his toy, and then have a game with you, after first complying with your 'Lie down' command. You may need to practise this for some time before he finally gets the message. Once he has, work on getting him to drop down on command when he is further and further away from you and nearer and nearer his toy.

4 If he will not stop and go down when you ask, put your foot on the long line and stop him this way.

Training tip

Do not do this 'down on the move' training more than twice a day maximum, however, or it will lose any sense of surprise and urgency in your dog's mind. Always end it as soon as you get a good response.

The mid-chase recall

This is a more advanced exercise that teaches your puppy not only to stop a chase, but also to come back to you, on your command.

1 Proceed as before with the 'down on the move' exercise (see page 67). This time, however, instead of allowing your puppy to go on to his toy, after he has stopped and lain down on your command, call him back to you.

2 When he comes back, make him sit and 'Wait' next to you for a few seconds.

3 Send him off to get his toy, asking him to 'Go get it!', then praise him really well when he brings it back to you, and play with it.

4 If your puppy will not come back to you, and he tries to move on, then reel him back in towards you on the line while repeating your recall command, e.g. 'Come!'

5 Make him sit and wait, and praise him for this, but immediately restart the exercise. He must learn that he will not get the toy until he responds as you ask.

Competitive events

Border Collies are such a clever, willing and versatile breed that owners may soon find themselves wondering whether they should channel their dogs' energies into pursuits such as Obedience, Agility or Flyball – either competitively or just as an enjoyable hobby.

Alternatively, you may feel you have such a good-looking Border Collie that you should exhibit him at 'breed' shows. So let us look now at what all these different pursuits may demand of your dog, and how you can get involved.

The Collie shown here is illustrating a perfect 'present' position, after a retrieve, of a kind and standard that is desirable in competitive Obedience.

Problems with training?

If you are experiencing any problems training your Border Collie, here are some of the commonest reasons why.

- You have not sufficiently taught him to respect your authority and concentrate on you when asked (see the 'Watch me' command on page 57)
- You have not made your commands clear enough, or sufficiently rewarding, for your dog to comply with consistently
- You are stressing/demoralizing your dog by being too harsh or oppressive in your tone of voice/body language or through making him do the same exercises again and again *ad nauseum*. Always keep all training sessions short and sweet and end on a positive, upbeat note with a game. Never train your dog when you are feeling tired, unwell or simply in a bad mood
- If the problems are occurring in training classes, it may well be that your dog is not suited to this kind of 'group learning' environment, and it would be better to seek professional one-to-one help with his training
- In general, never be afraid to seek expert professional advice, to help you get the very best out of an exceptionally bright dog.

Obedience

Competitive Obedience is a pursuit that requires you to train your dog to do set tasks and exercises in a ring in front of a judge. It is also one in which Border Collies tend to excel, if not totally dominate.

The set Obedience exercises become progressively more difficult, as well as demanding of total accuracy, as you 'win out' of one class and then progress up to another. At Open level, you would start your dog in a basic Pre-Beginners class before moving up to Beginners, then Novice, then A, B and C classes. The highest classes of all are those in which the 'C' competitors are vying for 'tickets' (Obedience Challenge Certificates). After a dog has amassed three such 'tickets' at Championship shows, he becomes an Obedience Champion.

What you have to do

Although the Obedience tasks you will be required to perform, and the degree of accuracy demanded, get more testing as you advance from one competitive level to the next, in total the exercises consist of the following:

- **Heelwork**: on and off the lead
- **Recall**: dog must return to the owner/handler on command.

Heelwork

Obedience heelwork is a beautiful illustration of dog and owner harmony in training, but also calls for immense precision. Begin from a neat sit position.

The dog must then move forward with his handler, staying tight and close to his/her leg as they follow a course of lines, turns and halts outlined by a judge.

Any 'crooked' sits by the dog, or his 'drifting' or moving off a fixed position on his handler's side will be penalized. This dog is doing it perfectly for his owner.

- **Retrieve:** initially with a dumbbell, then later with other articles of the judge's choosing.
- **Sit and down stays:** your dog must remain in the same position, on command, for a set time and even, at the more advanced level, while you leave the ring and go out of sight.
- **'Sendaway':** you must send your dog away to a fixed spot and then drop him down there, accurately, on command.

Retrieve

I A competitive Obedience retrieve exercise begins with the dog waiting while a specified item is thrown.

2 The dog is then sent by the owner or handler to retrieve the item – in this case, a dumbbell.

3 The dog must then pick up the item cleanly in his mouth and return swiftly with it to his handler.

4 Finally, the dog must 'present' the item to his handler, sitting very close and straight.

- **Distant control:** you must get your dog to change into set positions – down, sit or stand – on your command while he is some distance away from you.
- **Scent discrimination:** your dog must pick out a cloth with a specific scent from many other 'decoys' that are also laid out.

Getting started

The great thing about Obedience is that, whatever level you wish to take it to with your own Border Collie, your dog can only ever be better off for the training you put in. Likewise, the 'working bond' you build with him will get stronger and stronger. Most people get started in Obedience through their local dog training club. If your Collie shows a particular talent for Obedience, it may be worth getting further one-to-one help from an expert Obedience trainer to boost your progress (see page 126).

Distant control

The Distant Control exercise in Obedience requires the dog to change his position, on his handler's command, while some distance away from him or her.

The positions are 'sit', 'down' and 'stand', and the order in which these are given to a dog by a handler will be instructed by a judge.

If a dog gets a position wrong or moves more than a body length forward during the exercise, he will be penalized.

Agility and Flyball

Agility, or 'show jumping for dogs', as it is often referred to, is becoming an increasingly popular pursuit and one in which, once again, Border Collies dominate. Dogs compete with others to negotiate and clear a round of varied obstacles, such as jumps, tunnels, 'A' frames, weaving poles, hoops and seesaws, in the quickest time to win. Agility competitions are now so popular that sometimes hundreds of dogs will be entered in a class and placings will be decided on fractions of seconds.

In Flyball, dogs race in 'relay' teams over a line of hurdles, catch a ball at the end and then return with this, over the same hurdles, to their handlers. The team with the most clear rounds, in the fastest times, wins. Most people progress on to this exciting pursuit with their dogs through an Agility club.

Getting started

If you are interested in Agility, then your local training club can usually point you in the direction of an easily accessible Agility group/club if it does not run one itself (also see page 126). Be aware however, that many Agility clubs can have waiting lists to join, and that you will not be able to compete with your dog until he is 18 months old. With Agility, as with Obedience, you begin competing in the lowest (Elementary) classes and then gradually work your way up to the top Championship level. You also have to be quite fit, and your dog has to be suitably trained, in order to do well in this pursuit.

Border Collies love participating in Agility competitions with their owners. Agility helps keep them mentally and physically fit.

Showing

In recent years, a distinct division seems to have occurred between the typical 'working type' of pedigree Border Collie, i.e. highly athletic build, strong working instinct and 'eye'/supreme mental alertness, and the pedigree 'show' Border Collie, which now often tends to be a shorter-legged, less obviously athletic and far fluffier specimen.

How you feel about this depends on whether you are a purist like me, who believes that in any traditional working breed, the 'working type' of dog and the dog who wins prizes in the show ring should be one and the same thing.

The right 'look'

It's a fact of life, however, that if you want your Border Collie to do really well in the modern breed show ring, then he not only has to basically conform to the set 'Breed Standard' (see page 14) but he must also have the distinct type of 'look' and features that are currently fashionable among breed show judges. Dogs like this are best acquired from breeders who specialize in 'show' Border Collies.

Getting started

You can start showing your Border Collie from around the age of six months at Open 'breed' shows before, depending on his success, moving up to Championship shows where breed CCs (Challenge Certificates) are up for grabs. A dog who wins three breed CCs becomes a Show Champion.

To be successful in the show ring, you will have to learn how to groom, present and handle your dog to best effect. You can acquire this knowledge by attending your local Ringcraft classes. Contact the Kennel Club for details (see below).

Contact advice

The Kennel Club is the best organization to contact for details of local Training, Agility/Flyball and Ringcraft classes and clubs, plus websites that can provide more information on these subjects and forthcoming shows. They can also advise on how to get involved in other pursuits, such as Working Trials or Heelwork to Music (HTM). For more information and contact details, see page 100.

The weekly UK publications *Dog World* and *Our Dogs* advertise forthcoming breed shows, as well as 'Companion shows'. These are more informal events, where you can start your dog off in showing – and, frequently, Obedience – classes and simply enter on the day.

Border Collies must be Kennel Club or ISDS registered to compete at any KC-licensed breed show. If your dog is not a registered pedigree dog then, in order to compete in events like Obedience and Agility, you will need to put him on the KC's special Working Register.

Chapter 5

The adult dog

As your Border Collie grows into an adult dog, you should begin seeing the rewards of everything you got right, in terms of his rearing, socialization and training, while he was a puppy. Alternatively, of course, anything that was done wrong may come back to haunt you!

Adolescence

Whatever the case, adolescence (which typically runs from seven to 18 months of age) can still be a tricky phase for many dogs and their owners. As a new rush of sex hormones kicks in, Collies leave their puppy dependency behind to establish their adult identities, both in relation to other dogs and their surrounding world.

It is important not to panic or despair during this transitory period, as the consistent training and calm, authoritative handling outlined in the previous chapters should get most Collies through it with minimal trauma. If, however, adolescence triggers any behavioural changes in your dog that you find particularly worrying or disturbing, it is vital to seek professional help as soon as they begin. Do not wait

until they have become more serious problems, or ingrained habits. For more advice, turn to the next chapter on Behaviour (see page 88).

Dogs with a past

Many people rehome adult Border Collies or get one from a rescue centre. However, a lot of these dogs may come with 'baggage' – problems that are rooted in their past lives, including anything from inadequate early socialization and training to neglect or even ill treatment by their former owners. These behaviour problems will be covered in the next chapter (see page 88).

Exercise

You will often hear it said that adult Border Collies require a lot of exercise – and this is true – but the type of exercise is equally important. The best kind of physical daily exercise you can give your Collie, to maintain his health, fitness and stamina, is steady and prolonged off-lead and free-running distance work:

Opposite: Fit, happy and healthy adult Border Collies, in their physical and mental prime, are a true delight to own and to train.

a minimum of two walks per day in the morning and evening, which are at least an hour long.

Social skills and scentwork

Ideally, you should also give your dog ample opportunity to interact with other dogs and people on these daily outings. This will keep his social skills well honed. Make sure that you integrate different training exercises into your walks, too, to keep your dog mentally occupied and train him to respond to you in different situations and environments.

At home, you can give your dog lots of scentwork – getting him to find bits of food or different toys hidden around the house and garden. This will help keep him in a calmer frame of mind.

Warning

If you are tempted to skimp on the above kind of daily routine and instead limit your Collie's physical and mental exercise quota to just chasing and catching a ball for 15 or 20 minutes here or there, be warned: all this achieves is to get your dog hideously wound-up. Thereafter he will be far less likely to settle down again and more prone to injure himself. In addition, if he is endlessly chasing after a ball when you take him out, he is doing nothing to enhance or reinforce his social skills.

Opposite: Plenty of exercise, games and social interaction will keep your dog fit.

Develop a routine

A proper daily routine, such as the one that I have outlined here, of mental occupation and steady and prolonged physical exercise will help to keep a Border Collie not only healthy but also psychologically well balanced, and thus less likely to develop bad habits and behaviour problems that spring chiefly from boredom and frustration.

Obesity

Border Collies are a breed that can run to fat if their owners don't exert proper control over their daily exercise and food intake. Allowing a dog to become obese is not a by-product of 'love' but one of neglect. It not only totally destroys his everyday quality of life but it also greatly heightens his risk of suffering serious health problems and a shortened lifespan. So please make sure that you never let this happen to your dog.

Border Collies can vary considerably in their size and build, but typically bitches should weigh around 16–18kg and male dogs in he region of 18–21kg. As a general rule, you should easily be able to feel the outline of your dog's ribs as you run your hands down his sides. If you have any doubts about the correct weight for your Border Collie, or how to keep this within healthy limits, you should consult your vet and ask for advice. Many vets provide owners with diet sheets or even run special classes for obese dogs.

Diet

When Collies are growing, I generally advise putting them on a high-quality hypoallergenic (free of any additives or preservatives) dry 'complete' food. This ensures they get exactly the right balance of nutrients that are vital for healthy growth and development.

Once my dogs are mature, however, I substitute roughly half of this daily dried food ration with a mixture of fresh and raw food, i.e. around a heaped tablespoonful of raw meat (beef, lamb or tripe) or fish, such as trout or mackerel. My dogs' idea of heaven is a raw rainbow trout, complete with head and tail! I also sometimes give them raw offal (lamb's heart or liver), cooked white fish, or canned tuna or pilchards. I add raw vegetables (spinach, cabbage, carrots, broccoli or green beans – all mashed up first in a blender for greater ease of digestion) and pasta, rice or potatoes to their food. When available, they also get raw meaty beef bones.

I find this kind of varied diet keeps my dogs in tip-top condition – and likewise their teeth. The only meat I keep to a minimum with my dogs is chicken or turkey, as many Collies' digestive systems cannot tolerate too much of either. The same often goes for canned food.

Feeding your Collie a healthy, varied diet will keep him in top condition.

Grooming your dog

The coats of Border Collies can vary considerably in both their length and texture. In the main, however, they should always be brushed daily, and dogs with longer coats should have these thoroughly combed out once every two or three days. This is conducive to healthy skin, spreads oil through their coats and keeps them free of tangles, debris and loose hair.

Combing

When combing your dog, pay particular attention to the hair around the collar area, behind the ears, the 'breeching' above the back legs, and the entire tail region (including under the tail), as these are the areas where tangles and matting most often occur.

Brushing

When brushing your dog, start by vigorously brushing backwards, against the lie of the coat, i.e. from the root of the tail back to the neck, before brushing the coat back into place.

Note: Grooming your dog also gives you the opportunity to check him over for parasites, such as fleas or ticks, and any new lumps, bumps or swellings that should be reported to your vet and checked out without delay.

Begin grooming by vigorously, but not over-harshly, brushing your dog's coat backwards from tail to head to boost skin circulation and stimulate oils.

For the best results, you should always use only a good-quality bristle brush, rather than a synthetic one, when grooming your Border Collie.

Next, thoroughly comb out your dog's coat to remove any remaining matts, tangles or debris. Be gentle when combing out any knots you may find.

Pay particular attention to the area of thick hair behind your Border Collie's ears, which can get very matted. Do not force the comb through – be gentle.

You must also pay attention to your dog's tail area and the 'breeching' on his hind legs, which can get tangled or dirty. Comb through carefully.

A regular grooming regime like this will help to keep your dog's coat in top condition. You must make time for a grooming session at least twice a week.

Teeth

You should also clean and, if necessary, descale your dog's teeth regularly, as failure to do this can result in bad breath and gum disease. The latter will not only cause him much pain and discomfort but will also lead to other serious health problems as he gets older.

The best way to clean his teeth is with a brush dipped in some diluted bicarbonate of soda. Put a few pinches of the soda in a small bowl, then pour boiling water on to it and allow the mixture to cool. Using a special dog toothbrush, or soft baby's toothbrush bought from a chemist, gently clean

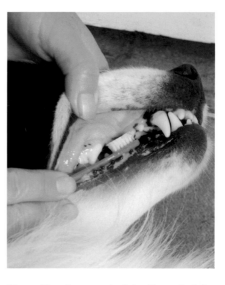

Below: Regularly giving your dog special hide chews will also help to keep his teeth and gums healthy. You can buy them in pet stores and supermarkets.

Above: Cleaning your dog's teeth regularly is vital to keep his breath sweet and prevent him suffering much pain and serious illness in later life.

Treats and training

To keep a responsive dog, never give your Collie any kind of treat until he has co-operated with one of your commands first.

This owner has taught her dog to sit and focus on her in return for a chew.

As soon as the dog sits in exactly the right position, he gets the treat.

around your dog's teeth with the mixture, paying special attention to the gum margins, and loosening and scraping any tartar off the teeth with a special scaling tool. This is available from many good pet stores and dog grooming suppliers.

The earlier, and more often, you do this, the quicker your dog will get used to it. Raw meaty bones, hide chews and other similar items from pet stores,

which are designed to promote chewing in dogs, should also help keep his teeth and gums in good shape.

Your dog's teeth have got to last him a lifetime, so never throw harder, heavier items, such as stones and rocks, for him to chase and catch, as these can break or severely damage his teeth. Many owners play games with sticks, but you should never throw these, as they can inflict appalling injuries on dogs.

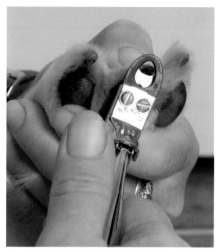

The pink nail 'quick' can be most easily seen in white-clawed Collies. If you cut this, it will bleed profusely.

Always employ caution in this exercise when cutting your Collie's claws – or, if you are nervous, leave it to your vet.

Claws

Your Border Collie's claws, including the special 'dew claws' inside his front legs, may need regular clipping to keep them short, blunt and strong. You must be careful, however, not to cut the 'quick' in any nail, as it will bleed profusely. An experienced owner or breeder will show you what to do. If you feel at all worried or squeamish about performing this task, then do not attempt it but ask your vet to do it for you.

Ears

Ear problems can cause Border Collies considerable pain and irritation, so regularly check that your dog's ears are healthy inside. Healthy ears should look clean and smell earthy and sweet. If, instead, they look inflamed, smell bad or show evidence of any discharge, this

suggests a possible infection. If you see a large build up of brown wax in your dog's ears, he may well have ear mites. Your vet can treat both these conditions.

Old age

Border Collies are usually a relatively long-lived breed, and one in which dogs living to 16 or 17 years old are not unusual. A good proportion of such longevity will be simply a result of good genes, but how well a dog's health and general welfare are looked after, throughout his life, is also critical.

Not allowing your Collie to become fat as he gets older, and keeping him fit with regular exercise and a good diet, are part of this all-important care, as are immediate veterinary check-ups should you spot any worrying physical or behavioural changes in your dog.

Signs of old age

Some progressive changes, however, are quite normal in older Border Collies, once they get beyond eight years of age. Their joints may move more stiffly, the hair around their muzzles and eyes can turn grey, their hearing may become less sharp and they can sometimes get a bit grumpy. Older Collies can also become more 'clingy' towards their owners, and more distressed by any sudden changes in their surroundings or routine.

Looking after the older dog

You must look after your senior citizen kindly and compassionately. It is likely that he has given you his all, throughout his earlier years, and now it is pay back time. If you observe your ageing Collie struggling, or trailing behind, on long

Believe it or not, this lively Collie is aged ten and a mother of two large litters – proof that looking after your dog well from day one will pay off in later life.

walks that he used to manage easily, cut his exercise back to around three shorter walks a day. This is enough to keep his joints mobile without over-taxing them, and also provides the ongoing mental stimulation that is vital for an older dog. Always ensure, additionally, that your older Collie has somewhere warm, dry, cosy and peaceful to rest and sleep whenever he needs to.

The passing of time, inevitably, takes a physical toll on any dog, but one of

Opposite: Another sprightly senior Collie citizen. This tricolour Border Collie bitch is aged 12 and still skipping miles over the fields each day.

the most remarkable things about Border Collies is that, even in old age, their sheer irrepressible spirit endures to the bitter end. As long as there is still one more ball to be caught, and a last imaginary cat to be chased out of the garden with their tails held high, they will keep on going.

Chapter 6

Behaviour

You may be lucky enough to own one or more Border Collies who never give you a moment's trouble. Alternatively, you may have always had 'easier' Collies like this but now acquired one who is far more difficult, in terms of his general personality or behaviour. This is not an uncommon occurrence, and, as outlined in the earlier chapters, results from some aspect of the dog's genetic make-up and/or his early rearing, socialization and training which have made him struggle harder with the demands of 'pet life'. If you have taken on a rescued adult Border Collie, as opposed to a puppy, there can also be a higher chance of him possessing some problem behaviours.

Either way, exactly why common 'problem behaviours' occur in Border Collies, and what their owners can do about them, are examined in this chapter.

Genetic make-up

I have already stressed the importance of getting your Border Collie from the right kind of breeding background, and seeing as many of his immediate relatives as possible, to establish what their 'typical' personalities are like. This is because the genetic make-up of any

individual dog will govern so many different aspects of his 'natural' temperament and character – from how strong his eye/stalk/chase/herd/ nip (or 'working') instincts are to how prone he may be to more obsessive, fearful, defensive or reactive patterns of behaviour.

Early rearing

If, on top of the more testing character leanings, cited above, a Border Collie is not raised, socialized and trained correctly (as outlined in the previous chapters) to best 'fit' the lifestyle of a social companion for which he is destined, then the capacity for his behaviour to become a problem can be magnified even further.

Chase behaviour

Inappropriate chase behaviour – or dogs targeting their eye/stalk/chase instincts onto inappropriate things, e.g. traffic, runners, cyclists or other dogs – is one of the commonest sources of frustration

Opposite: A good understanding of the unique instincts, energies and psychology of the Border Collie is vital in the management of these dogs as problem-free pets.

and despair for Border Collie owners. They may often think that the stalking/chasing itself is a 'behaviour problem' in their dog, when it is really a completely natural part of a Border Collie's genetic behaviour. The 'problem' is that it has become directed on to all the wrong targets, for want of better training earlier on in the dog's life.

In order to better control this type of behaviour, you will need to work much harder on getting your dog's focus directed chiefly on to you, and his toys,

Above: In order to best control your Border Collie, you, and his toys – rather than any other surrounding distractions or targets – have to become the main focus of his obsessive working drives and instincts. And the earlier that you begin this conditioning process, the better the results should be.

and then you must do some relentless anti-chase training with him (see page 67). You can get some additional help with this from a professional trainer if you think that it is needed. For more information see page 126.

Some Border Collies will chase cyclists and lunge out at them, but this inappropriate behaviour can be treated successfully.

Lunging and nipping

Border Collies who lunge out and attempt to nip things like passing traffic, people or dogs are another example of natural working behaviour going awry. The lunge/nip reflex is actually a vital instinct in sheepdogs to head off possible attacks or challenges by livestock.

Some dogs will always activate it more readily, strongly or inappropriately than others, particularly if they have lower social confidence, or are more genetically inclined to this behaviour. Alternatively they may just discover that they get a 'buzz' from the habit, which they want to keep repeating. The best way to deal with this behaviour is to

Train your dog to sit and 'watch' you and to wait for a rewarding tasty treat or toy in a potential lunging situation.

train your dog to 'watch' you, in return for a rewarding toy or a tasty treat (see page 57) every time a potential 'lunging target' goes by. If this does not work, however, then an additional deterrent may also be needed.

Psychological problems

Misapplied working instincts apart, some Collies can still have a heightened genetic tendency towards the following:
• Fearfulness and phobias
• Nervous and defensive reactions
• Obsessive-compulsive patterns of behaviour
• Manic or over-excitable behaviour.
These, alas, can be the psychological downsides of genetically favouring dogs, for generations, with hypersensitive minds and reactions and an obsessive attitude to work.

Such psychological problems, however, can be greatly exacerbated by such factors as poor early socialization or inappropriate owner handling, and they have different

triggers and roots in individual dogs. This is why expert help is always recommended to get to the heart of the problem, and thereafter find the best possible solutions for each dog concerned.

Boredom and anxiety behaviours

Behaviours such as digging, incessant barking and destructiveness are common ways in which Collies externalize their boredom, frustration or anxiety, particularly if they are under-exercised, under-stimulated, or are left alone by their owners for long periods.

Not all dogs have a 'pack mentality', but Collies are a breed that definitely does, and thus they cope less well with being separated from their owners for lengthy spells of time. They are also more easily bored than other dogs, and

the progression thereafter to frustration and anxiety can be short. Many obsessive behaviour patterns in Collies, such as endlessly repetitive cycles of eyeing/stalking/chasing different objects, also only originate, or escalate, as a result of some ongoing source of stress and frustration, including their energies not being better channelled elsewhere.

If you train your Border Collie from puppyhood to cope with being left for occasional periods on his own, he will be less likely to develop problems when he is left as an adult. However, there is still a limit to how long any Collie should be expected to remain confined on his own without resorting to tension-releasing behaviour. If you must leave him for longer than two hours at a stretch, get a dog sitter or minder to regularly look in on him or stay with him for company. Also, always ensure you have exercised your dog well before leaving him.

Rescue dog problems

Over and above any commoner quirks of behaviour to which Collies may be prone as a breed, dogs who are rehomed or are acquired from rescue centres may have additional problems which relate to their past lives. Many may be highly stressed from previous confinement in kennels, or find it initially hard to establish good and trusting relationships with people, which will affect how successfully or quickly you can train them.

Boredom and frustration can be the triggers for many of the less desirable behaviours in Collies, so make sure that you keep your dog occupied.

Some Border Collies will take time to build a bond of trust with people.

in the past to deal with these things. The new owners, by contrast, feel that they have given the dog their love and a new life, and his 'bad' behaviour, in return, indicates his 'ingratitude'.

It is important to understand the troubled psychology of a dog who has basically lost his way in life and is struggling to regain it. What dogs like this mostly crave is some real sense of security and continuity in their lives. The best way to do this is with some classic 'tough love', i.e. establishing your authority and some firm daily rules and routines and consistently making your dog comply with them all.

Others may have become excessively insecure, which can manifest itself in the dog showing timid and retiring behaviour, or destructive and manic behaviour. He may even try to overcompensate and rule his new roost with strategies varying from constant attention-seeking ploys to intimidation through aggression.

Tough love

One of the commonest reasons why things go wrong between rescue dogs and their new owners in the early days is because they are working to such different, and often highly conflicting, emotional agendas. When dogs go to new homes they often cannot think beyond their own immediate anxieties and insecurities, which makes them resort to the coping strategies (as previously described) they have used

Addressing problems

If you are experiencing any kind of problem with your Border Collie's behaviour, it's important to address it correctly the instant it starts and go through the following checklist. This is particularly imperative if your dog's problem is aggression.

- First, take your dog to the vet for a full check-up. There could be a medical reason behind the problem, especially if the behaviour has come on suddenly
- Is your dog on medication? This could affect his behaviour. Ask your vet
- Have you been giving your dog any food or treats containing artificial colourings, additives or flavourings? If so, stop, as these can have an adverse impact on many Collies' behaviour
- Are you giving your dog ample physical and mental exercise each day? If not, he may just be highly stressed or frustrated

- Are you leaving your dog alone for long periods? The same applies
- Have there been any recent changes or upheavals in your dog's living environment, i.e. a house move, relationship split, builders coming, ill health, bereavement, a new dog or baby? All these things can have a significant impact on dogs and their sense of security
- Make notes of when your dog's 'problem' behaviour first began, what things have triggered it since, and as many other relevant details as possible. This will be really useful if you seek professional advice
- Consult professional help

Professional help

When people's cars or washing machines go wrong, the first thing they do is to find a person who knows about these things to fix them. When owners have problems with their dogs, however, they can go through extraordinary long periods of denial, and highly stressful 'muddling through', before eventually seeking the same kind of solution.

This may be due to the frailties of the human ego in some part, but it is also really counterproductive thinking, because not only do very few problems with dogs ever get better without expert help, but most actually get worse through being handled inappropriately.

By trying to 'go it alone', owners may also look for quick fixes to complex problems in the shape of different deterrent devices, such as remote control spray collars, or worse. These gadgets,

alas, rely on a fair degree of skill and knowledge to operate effectively.

If you do not fully understand how dogs learn, or how critical it is to match, with pinpoint accuracy, the timing and association of their use in your Border Collie's mind, then not only will you not solve his problem but you could also create an awful lot more that he did not have before your clumsy attempt at treatment.

Finding the right expert

When looking for your own 'expert' be careful, as, sadly, there are too many cowboys operating today. The person you choose should ideally have plenty of experience with Border Collies, use only kind methods and belong to a recognized professional body. In Britain, you could contact the UK Registry of Canine Behaviourists, the Association of Pet Behaviour Counsellors or the Association of Pet Dog Trainers (see page 126).

Finding someone via your vet, or by personal recommendation, is often the best way but, even so, still ask for the contact numbers of past clients to check that this person really is right for you and your dog. Depending on the level of expert you use, their services could be quite expensive, even for a single session, but often you can get such fees partly or wholly covered by your pet insurance scheme, so check this out in advance.

Also be aware that a dog expert can only advise and illustrate what you should be doing to alter or modify your dog's behaviour. It is you who will have to stick to, and work hard at, what has

been advised on a daily basis, in order to see any improvement in your dog. Such improvement can still take time to fully materialize, so you will have to be dedicated and patient.

The author and her three beloved Border Collies: Arun, Ilona and Lara.

Last words

The main aim of this book has been to give the reader as accurate and honest a picture possible of the Border Collie breed, explore how they unfairly gained a reputation for being 'problem pets' and to explain how to get only the very best out of them as companions.

From the moment I got my first Border Collie, many years ago, I knew that this was the only breed for me. I also know that I am not alone in this sentiment as, day after day, I have owners tell me about the Border Collies

they have loved and lost years or even decades ago, and whom they still mourn and can never replace.

These dogs have a way of not just taking over your life but also of working their way into your soul. Once they have made that all-important bond with you, they will be your ever-willing work mate, tireless shadow and most trusted and constant of friends.

They will even know what you are thinking as you think it. They will predict what you are going to do before you do it. Sometimes they can be mad and other times they can be bad but, to my mind at least, you will still never, ever, own another breed like them.

PART TWO

HEALTHCARE

As a good owner, it is your responsibility to keep your Border Collie fit and healthy. If you follow the basic guidelines in this book and socialize him, feed him a nutritious diet, exercise him adequately, groom him and play with him, you can prevent many health problems. However, it is important that you learn to recognize the warning signs of common problems and diseases so that you can treat them yourself or seek professional help from your vet before they get worse. Prevention is always preferable to cure, and a healthy, contented dog will be your trusted companion for many years to come.

Signs of good health

Coat The coat should be in good condition and should smell pleasantly 'doggy'. It should be glossy and pleasant to touch. When you part the hairs, there should be no signs of fleas' droppings, sore or bare patches.

Anal region This should be clean without faeces clinging to the fur. The dog should not lick this area excessively or drag his rear along the ground.

Eyes The eyes should be bright, alert and with no signs of discharge, swelling or tear stains. A tiny amount of 'sleep' in the inner corners is quite normal.

Ears They should be responsive to any sound. The insides should be pale pink with no visible wax or unpleasant smell. Your dog should not shake his head or scratch his ears too often.

Nose The nose of a healthy dog should be cold and damp without any discharge. Occasionally there may be a little clear fluid.

Teeth Healthy teeth are white and smooth, not yellow, which can be a sign of plaque and tartar formation. The breath should not smell unpleasant and there should be no loose or missing teeth or inflamed or bleeding gums.

Claws The claws should end level with the pad and not be too long. Look out for broken claws, damage to dew claws (if they have not been removed) and hay seeds embedded in the pads. Border Collies have oval-shaped paws and, as a result, the two middle claws on each foot – particularly the front ones – may bear less weight and have less wear than the side ones, and may need clipping or filing more often.

Body The dog's body should be firm and well-muscled. He should not carry excess weight nor be so thin that his ribs stick out.

Hereditary diseases

As in humans, Border Collies can inherit a number of diseases. They are caused by genetic faults or aberrations in breeding lines. The genetic background to many hereditary ailments can be extremely complicated and is of concern to all professional breeders, veterinarians and geneticists as well as owners.

Screening tests are available for tendencies to some hereditary diseases, and potential owners of dogs should consult their vet about possible inherited health problems within the breed and ask the breeder about the lineage and history of the dams and sires before purchasing a puppy. Although some hereditary diseases are treatable, the underlying genetic faults cannot be eliminated.

Hip dysplasia

This is one of the most common inherited diseases in dogs. In a normal, healthy dog the hip is a 'ball and socket' joint, which allows a wide range of movement. The rounded end at the top of the femur fits tightly into the cup-shaped socket in the pelvis. In hip dysplasia, a shallow socket develops with a distorted femur head and slack joint ligaments. There can be excessive movement between the femur and pelvis, leading to a malfunctioning joint which will gradually become arthritic.

Early symptoms

If a puppy develops severe hip dysplasia he may have difficulty walking. Getting up from a sitting position may be painful and he will cry out. When he runs, he may use both hind legs together in a 'bunny hop' or look as though he is swaying.

These symptoms may be identifiable from five months onwards. Mildly affected puppies may show no signs at all of hip dysplasia at this age, but they will begin to develop arthritis later on in life at about eight years of age.

Hip dysplasia scheme

The British Veterinary Association and the Kennel Club run a joint scheme (the BVA/KC hip dysplasia scheme) based on hip scoring. The vet submits the X-ray, bearing the KC registration number of the dog, to the scheme. Each hip is then scored by a veterinary radiologist from 0 to 54, making a total of 108 maximum between the two hips. The lower the score the better, and 0:0 is the best score possible. The average score for Border Collies is 13, so anything less than that is excellent.

You should not breed from a dog or bitch with a higher hip score than the average or hip dysplasia will never be reduced or eliminated from the breed. When buying a puppy, check that both parents have been X-rayed, scored, and achieved a low score. This does not guarantee the puppy won't develop hip dysplasia but it does reduce the chances.

Treatment If mild hip dysplasia is treated in a growing puppy with anabolic steroids, limited exercise and diet, he will often grow into a healthy adult dog. However, you may have to restrict his exercise later on, too. In severe cases, surgery is available.

Osteochondritis dessicans

This is another condition of the skeleton, which is sometimes seen in Border Collies. Faulty nutrition together with genetic factors are responsible for this degeneration of the cartilage in the joints of dogs aged between four and 18 months. Lameness results, which, if left untreated, can become permanent. Diagnosis is by X-ray, and treatment involves rest, surgery and, less frequently, medication.

Other hereditary problems

Even though, in the main, Border Collies are genetically a relatively healthy breed, there has been evidence of some of the conditions described below.

Epilepsy

Like other breeds, Border Collies can suffer from epilepsy, resulting from such things as an underactive thyroid, distemper virus, brain tumours, toxins such as lead, arsenic, poisonous plants, parasites and trauma, but there is also an inherited form. Symptoms include collapse, uncontrolled leg movements and rigid seizures. After determining the cause in any particular case, the vet can advise on treatment by medication.

Ceroid Lipofuscinosis (CL or Batten's Disease)

A rare disease of Border Collies (some other breeds, cattle, sheep, cats and humans are also affected), CL is a progressive degeneration of brain and eye cells, which can develop in dogs of 16–24 months old. Symptoms include muscle weakness, seizures and cognitive dysfunction. Affected Collies rarely survive much beyond two years.

A DNA test is now available in many countries for detecting the gene behind the disease. There is no treatment or cure yet available.

Trapped Neutrophil Syndrome (TNS)

This newly-recognized and difficult to diagnose disease of Border Collies is a rare inherited disorder of the immune system, which can produce a variety of symptoms, including inappetance, poor growth, vomiting, fever and lameness in puppies as young as two weeks and is invariably fatal. It can resemble 'fading puppy syndrome'.

Most of the research into this problem is being carried out in Australia and New Zealand. A DNA test to detect carriers is being perfected, but there is, currently, no form of treatment.

Exercise-Induced Hyperthermia (EIH) and Malignant Hyperthermia (MH)

EIH occurs during warm weather when the dog heats up while he is exercising. The symptoms include staggering, seizures and collapse and they usually last around 15 minutes. MH can occur not just when it is hot, however, and dogs that are prone to it can develop dangerously high temperatures if under anaesthetic.

Sudden Collapse Syndrome

This is where a Border Collie collapses after a short period of exercise and soon recovers, but it is not well understood. It may be related to the Hyperthermia conditions described above (see page 101). There is no treatment, although some experts have recommended ensuring that there is enough potassium in the dog's diet.

MDR gene

Collies can also have a fault in the MDR (Multi drug resistant) gene, which means that toxins, including some medications, like ivermectin, that would otherwise be pumped away from the brain, enter it, as a result of them having a more permeable brain membrane. In dogs with this condition, care must be taken when prescribing medication.

Skin problems

Collies can also occasionally suffer skin problems, sometimes allergies, but also, in certain lines, there is a tendency to suffer badly from demodectic mange and fleas. The problem is not really the mange mites or fleas,which can be tackled by modern anti-parasitic medication, but an immune system which reacts excessively to the invaders.

Digestive problems

Some Border Collies have sensitive digestions, making them more prone to colitis, resulting in a tendency to diarrhoea and flatulence. Usually, the problem is best controlled by finding the most appropriate diet for them, often containing more fibre.

Eye conditions

Certain important eye conditions can be found in Border Collies and they will necessitate immediate veterinary advice. They include the following problems as listed below.

Collie Eye Anomaly (CEA)

This is a congenital, inherited disease of both eyes which is caused by improper development of the organs and involving their deep and superficial tissues. Blindness follows in severe cases. It can be diagnosed opthalmoscopically from the age of six to seven weeks. Most good breeders will have their litters tested for this condition before selling you a puppy. Recently a genetic test has been developed in the USA that can identify affected animals and those carrying the disease that are as yet free of symptoms. There is no treatment.

Corneal dystrophy

This is the development of greyish deposits of fat and calcium within the corneas of both eyes, usually at between two and four years of age. Vision is not affected and treatment is unnecessary.

Primary Lens Luxation (PLL)

This involves dislocation of the lens of the eye, so that it rests in an abnormal position. It can be primary, an inherited condition of puppies, or may be acquired later in life through trauma or other eye disease. The primary form is common in Border Collies. It can result in glaucoma, pain, reduced vision and, eventually, blindness. Treatment is by surgery.

Central progressive retinal atrophy (PRA)

Dogs between three and five years with this condition begin to have difficulty seeing stationary objects and apparently see best in dim light. Both eyes are affected. The condition usually leads to complete blindness after a year or two. There is no effective treatment, but PRA can, and should, be tested for in adult dogs before breeding from them.

Congenital deafness

In Border Collies, this is caused by a gene linked to the gene responsible for areas of white in the animal's coat. The larger the amount of white in the dog's coat, the higher the chance of him being deaf. Owners can compensate for their dog's deafness by the use of hand signals. Experts who specialize in training deaf dogs could also prove to be very useful to you on this front, and their details should be found through other training advice organizations listed at the end of this book.

> **Note:** Veterinary treatment can ameliorate some of these conditions to some degree but cannot cure them. Tests (by ophthalmoscopy or DNA testing) are now available for screening puppies and adult dogs for some conditions.

Preventing disease

Prevention is always better than cure and there is a lot you can do to prevent diseases and health problems developing by keeping your dog in first-class condition. Get into the habit of inspecting and looking after his ears, eyes, teeth, coat, paws and rear end.

Check your dog

Check your dog over on a regular basis. A grooming session provides a good opportunity to examine your dog.
1 Look inside his mouth, checking that his teeth are clean and white and his breath does not smell unpleasant. Clean the teeth with special toothpaste or diluted bicarbonate of soda at least once a week.
2 Next check his eyes, nose and ears for any signs of discharge, odour or inflammation. Keep them clean by wiping them gently with some damp cotton wool.
3 Examine the dog's coat, looking for bald patches, excessive hair loss, tell-tale signs of fleas (black sooty specks in the fur) and soiling around the anus and rear end. The coat should look healthy and glossy, and the dog should not scratch excessively.
4 Pick up each of his paws and check the pads and claws, which should not be broken nor too long. If your dog appears to be limping, look for cuts or any swellings on the pads. Some dog breeds are susceptible to grass and hay seeds becoming embedded in their pads.

Vaccinations

The most important thing you can do to protect your dog's health is to make sure that he is vaccinated against the major infectious canine diseases. These are distemper, infectious canine hepatitis, 'kennel cough', parvovirus and the two forms of leptospirosis. Vaccination against all these serious ailments can be given by your vet in one shot when a puppy is at least six weeks of age. A second dose is administered three to six weeks later. An annual booster dose is recommended thereafter to top up your dog's immunity, although some veterinary authorities believe this is not necessary. However, like most vets, I personally am in favour of it.

In some countries vaccination of dogs against rabies is obligatory. Puppies can be vaccinated as early as four weeks of age. Yearly booster shots are essential.

Pet Passports

If you are considering taking your dog on holiday to one of the European Union countries or to certain other designated rabies-free countries, you must obtain a Pet Passport. The same applies to dogs travelling abroad to dog shows and competitive events. Your vet and the local DEFRA office will give you information on how to go about this. The dog will have to be micro-chipped, vaccinated against rabies and blood tested 30 days after vaccination before you leave for your trip, and then treated against ticks and other parasites 24 to 48 hours before your return with a veterinary certificate to prove it. You must have a DEFRA PETS re-entry certificate certifying that the blood test gave a positive result for immunity against rabies after the vaccination, and you will have to sign a declaration that the dog did not leave the qualifying countries while you were away.

Neutering your dog

Unless you are definitely contemplating breeding from your dog, it is best, for your pet and for you, to have a bitch spayed or a dog castrated after they reach six months of age. Castration may reduce aggressiveness and the likelihood of a dog going a-roaming. Spaying, apart from avoiding the arrival of unwanted puppies, reduces the chances of breast tumours in later life and, obviously, the onset of common uterine disease, such as pyometra. I do not believe that castration or spaying changes the character of dogs nor necessarily makes them put on weight. However, talk to your vet about what is involved before deciding whether to go ahead.

Cryptorchidism

This is an inherited condition where one or both testicles have not descended by the time the pup is six months old, and is not uncommon in Border Collies. An undescended testicle is non-functional but a potential source of problems later in life, particularly of becoming cancerous. Removal of both testicles by surgical castration is recommended.

Diet is important

Feeding a balanced, nutritious diet will help to keep your Border Collie healthy. It is important not to over-feed him or he may gain too much weight and this can lead to many health problems that are associated with obesity (see page 116) as well as a reduced life expectancy.

If you are unsure as to which foods, how much and how often to feed your dog, ask your veterinary surgeon or breeder for advice. Similarly, if your dog loses his appetite or sheds weight suddenly, consult your vet – he may well need worming (see page 106) or the symptoms may be a sign of a more serious underlying problem. If this is the case, seek professional help.

Keep your dog fit

All dogs need regular exercise every day to keep fit and stay in optimum health, but an active working breed like the Border Collie should walk and run several miles a day, if possible, in order to maintain peak condition.

Stimulate your dog

Playing games with your dog and teaching him tricks will provide both mental and physical stimulation. Lively dogs like Border Collies need to be busy and active, or they soon become bored and this can lead to behaviour problems as well as to poor health.

Note: If you find anything unusual or suspect that there may be a health problem, then make an appointment to take your dog to the vet. Even if it is only a minor worry, this will set your mind at rest. You can treat the problem before it gets more serious as well as learning how to prevent it recurring in the future.

Parasites

External parasites

These parasites live on the surface of the dog's body, and include fleas, ticks and lice (see below) and mites and ringworm (see page 117). Look out for them and treat an infected dog as soon as possible

Fleas

Dogs are usually infested by their own, and the cat's, species of flea but sometimes they can carry rabbit, human or hedgehog fleas. The infestations are more likely to be worse in warm weather in the summer, but fleas thrive all the year round, particularly if your home

has central heating. Sometimes it is extremely difficult to find any fleas on a dog, but just a single flea can cause an allergic reaction when piercing a dog's skin and injecting its saliva. Such a reaction can result in widespread irritation, skin sores and rashes. Flea eggs do not stick to the dog's hair like those of lice but, being dry, they drop off onto carpets and furniture.

What you can do Use insecticidal sprays, shampoos or powders, which are obtainable from the vet, chemist or a pet shop, at regular intervals throughout the summer. Treat the floors, furniture and your pet's favourite sleeping places, basket and bedding with a specially formulated aerosol product every seven months. This procedure effectively stops the re-infestation of dogs by larvae emerging from eggs in the environment.

Lice

There are two kinds of lice – biting lice which feed on skin scales; and sucking lice which draw tissue fluids from the skin. The latter cause more irritation to the dog than the former. Lice are greyish-white and about 2mm ($1/8$in) in length. Their eggs (nits) are white and cemented to the dog's hairs. The dog louse does not fancy humans or cats and will not infest them.

> **COMMON SYMPTOMS**
> • **The dog will scratch himself**
> • **Lice and nits will be visible to the naked eye when the dog's coat is carefully searched.**

What you can do Sprays, powders or baths are available from the vet or pet shop. Apply on at least three occasions at five- to seven-day intervals to kill adults and the larvae that hatch from the nits.

Ticks

More often seen on country dogs than town dogs, ticks suck blood, their abdomen swelling up as they do so. The commonest tick of dogs is the sheep tick. It clings to the dog's hair, generally on the legs, head or under-belly, and pierces the skin with its mouth parts.

In doing so it can transmit an organism called Borrelia, a cause of Lyme Disease. Characterized by lameness and heart disease, it requires veterinary diagnosis by means of blood tests, and then treatment using specific antibiotics and anti-inflammatory drugs.

Specialist tick tweezers are useful for removing these little beasts. Avoid squashing the tick and releasing its fluids or leaving any part of the head in the skin as both may cause infection. Afterwards use some disinfectant on the affected area.

What you can do Remove a tick by dabbing it with some alcohol, such as gin or methylated spirits, waiting a few minutes for its head to relax, and then grasping it near to the mouthparts with fine tweezers. Dislodge the tick with a little jerk. Do not ever pull it off without applying alcohol first as the mouthparts left in the skin may cause an abscess.

An alternative method is to spray the tick with some flea spray and then to remove it the following day. The regular application of a flea spray or fitting your dog with an insecticidal collar during the summer months is highly recommended in order to control tick infestation.

Internal parasites

These parasites live inside the dog's body. Several kinds of worm can infest dogs and, in very rare cases, these parasites can spread to human beings.

Roundworms

These live, when adult, in the dog's intestines but their immature forms migrate through their host's body, damaging such organs as the liver and lungs, particularly those of puppies.

Hookworms and whipworms
These blood-sucking parasites can cause severe anaemia. Your vet will be able to confirm if your dog is affected.

Tapeworms and roundworms
The commonest dog tapeworm, Dipylidium, is spread by fleas, in which its larvae develop. The segments of this tapeworm look like wriggling white grains of rice in droppings or stuck

> **COMMON SYMPTOMS**
> • **Scratching**
> • **Tiny reddish scabs or papules appear on the skin, particularly on the dog's back**
> • **Flea droppings look like coal dust in the coat.**

to the hair around the dog's bottom. Roundworms cause the most trouble for dogs, particularly puppies.

What you can do To treat roundworms you should give your dog a 'worming' medication which will be available from your vet. Puppies usually should receive their first dose at three weeks of age. Repeat the worming every three weeks until they are 16 weeks old, repeating at six months and twice a year thereafter. Give your dog anti-tapeworm medication once a year or when any worm segments are seen in his droppings or on the hair near and around the anus.

Regular flea control will also help you to combat tapeworms. Some worm treatments are effective against all types of internal parasites, and you should consult your veterinary surgeon about which products are suitable and the correct dosage.

Dental care

It is easy to spot the common symptoms of tooth disease and dental decay. Cleaning the teeth once or twice weekly

> **COMMON SYMPTOMS**
> • **Your dog may salivate (slavering) at the mouth**
> • **He may paw at his mouth**
> • **His chewing motions may be exaggerated**
> • **He may chew tentatively as if he is dealing with a hot potato**
> • **His breath may smell unpleasant.**

with cotton wool or a soft toothbrush dipped in salt water (or specially formulated dog toothpaste) will stop tartar formation. 'Bones' and 'chews' made of processed hide (available from pet shops) and the occasional meal of coarse-cut, raw butcher's meat also helps.

Tartar
When tartar, a yellowy-brown, cement-like substance, accumulates, it does not produce holes in the teeth that need filling. Instead it damages the gum edge,

lets in bacteria to infect the tooth sockets and thus loosens the teeth. Tartar always causes some gum inflammation (gingivitis) and frequently bad breath.

If your pet displays the symptoms described, open his mouth and look for a foreign body stuck between his teeth. This may be a sliver of wood or bone stuck between two adjacent molars at the back of the mouth or a bigger object jammed across the upper teeth against the hard palate. You can usually flick out foreign bodies with a teaspoon handle.

Gingivitis (gum disease)

Bright red edging to the gums where they meet the teeth, together with ready bleeding on even gentle pressure, are the principal signs of gingivitis. Tap each tooth with your finger or a pencil. If there are any signs of looseness or tenderness, wash the dog's mouth with some warm water and salt, and give him an aspirin tablet – there is little else you can do without professional help. Take the dog to the vet and ask his advice.

Broken teeth

Sometimes a dog will break a tooth, perhaps by fighting or chewing stones (a bad habit that some dogs get into). The large 'fang' teeth (canines) are most often the ones damaged. These injuries do not usually produce any signs of toothache, root infection or death of the tooth. Treatments used in human dentistry, such as fillings, root treatments or crowning, may be necessary.

Ulcers and tumours

Mouth ulcers, tumours (juvenile warts are common in young dogs) and tonsillitis will all need veterinary diagnosis and treatment where they are the cause of some of the symptoms mentioned above.

Eye problems

Your dog's eyes are precious and thus you must check regularly that they are normal and healthy.

COMMON SYMPTOMS
- Sore, runny or 'mattery' eyes
- Blue or white film over the eye
- Partially or totally closed eye(s).

Watering and discharge

If just one of the dog's eyes is involved and the only symptom is watering or a sticky discharge without any marked irritation, you can try washing the eye gently with boracic acid powder in warm water once every few hours, followed by the introduction of a little Golden Eye ointment (which is obtainable from the chemist) onto the affected eyeball.

If any symptoms in or around the eyes last for more than a day, you must take the patient to the veterinary clinic and get professional treatment. Particularly in young dogs, two mattery eyes may indicate distemper (see page 111).

Eye conditions

Persistent watering of one or both eyes can be due to a very slight infolding of the eyelid, or to blocked tear ducts. A blue or white film over one or both eyes is normally a sign of keratitis, which is an inflammation of the cornea. This is not a cataract but it does require immediate veterinary attention.

Opacity of the lens (cataract) can be seen as a blue or white 'film' much deeper in the eye. The pupil looks greyish in colour instead of the usual black. This usually occurs in elderly dogs but it may be seen sometimes in young puppies (congenital cataract) and also at other ages (diabetic cataract).

Inflammations of the eye

These can be treated in various ways. Antibiotic injections, ointments and drops are available, plus other drugs to reduce inflammation, as are surgical methods of tackling ulcerated eyes under local anaesthesia. Problems due to deformed eyelids, foreign bodies embedded in the eyeball and even some cataracts can all be treated surgically.

Entropion

In this inherited disease the edge of the eyelid folds inwards so the lashes rub against the eyeball. The eye becomes sore and weeps and may be kept closed. The condition can be corrected with surgery.

Ear problems

A healthy dog's ears should be alert and responsive to sounds. The ear flaps of Border Collies are usually pale pink and silky inside, and there should be no wax or nasty odour. A dog who keeps scratching his ears and shaking his head may have an ear infection.

> **COMMON SYMPTOMS**
> - **Shaking the head and scratching the ear**
> - **It is painful when the ear is touched**
> - **There may be a bad smell and discharge**
> - **The dog tilts his head to one side**
> - **There is ballooning of the ear flap.**

Preventing problems

Clean your dog's ears once a week. For dogs with hair growing in the ear canal, pluck out the hair between finger and thumb. Don't cut it. Using 'baby buds' or twists of cotton wool moistened in warm olive oil, clean the ear with a twisting action to remove excess brown ear wax. See the vet early with any ear trouble. Chronic ear complaints can be very difficult to eradicate.

Treating minor problems

If symptoms suddenly appear and the dog is in distress, an effective emergency treatment is to pour a little warmed (not hot) liquid paraffin carefully into the affected ear. Acute inflammation will be greatly soothed by the oil. Don't stuff proprietary liquids into a dog's ear; you do not know what you may be treating. Most of all, avoid those so-called canker powders as the powder bases of these products can cause additional irritation by forming annoying accumulations that act as foreign bodies.

Ear irritation
This may be due to various things that find their way into the ear canal. Grass awns (pointed seed heads) may need professional removal. Small, barely visible white mange mites that live in dog's ears cause itching, and bacteria can set up secondary infections. Sweaty, dirty conditions, provide an ideal opportunity for germs to multiply, but Collies' ears are generally well ventilated, compared to breeds like spaniels, and contract ear problems much less frequently.

The vet will decide whether mites, bacteria, fungi or other causes are the source of inflammation, and will use appropriate antiparasitic, antibiotic or antifungal drugs as drops or injections.

Middle-ear disease
Although tilting of the head may be due simply to severe irritation on one side, it can indicate that the middle ear, the deeper part beyond the eardrum, is involved. Middle-ear disease does not necessarily result from outer-ear infection but may arise from trouble in the Eustachian tube which links the middle ear to the throat.

Middle-ear disease will always require some rigorous veterinary attention with the use of antiflammatory drugs, antibiotics and, more rarely, deep drainage operations.

Ballooning of an ear flap
This may look dramatic and serious but in fact it is a relatively minor problem. It is really a big blood blister, which is caused by the rupture of a blood vessel in the ear flap. It generally follows either some vigorous scratching where ear irritation exists or a bite from another dog.

It can be treated surgically by the vet, who may drain it with a syringe or open it and then stitch the ear flap in a special way to prevent any further trouble.

Nose problems

Don't allow your dog's nostrils ever to get caked and clogged up. Bathe them thoroughly with warm water and anoint the nose pad with some soothing cold cream. If there are any 'common cold' symptoms, you must seek veterinary advice immediately.

Sore noses
Old dogs with cracked, dry nose pads need regular attention to keep their

> **COMMON SYMPTOMS**
> - **The dog's nostrils are running and mattery**
> - **The dog appears to have the equivalent of a human common cold**
> - **The nose tip is sore, cracked and dry**
> - **Check the eyes as well as the nose – if they are both mattery, the dog may have distemper.**

nostrils free and to deal with bleeding from the cracks. You should bathe the nose frequently, applying cod liver oil ointment twice or three times daily and working it in well. Your vet may also prescribe multivitamins or corticosteroid preparations.

Rhinitis and sinusitis

Sneezing, a mattery discharge from the nostrils, head shaking and, perhaps, nose bleed may indicate rhinitis (the inflammation of the nasal passages) or sinusitis (inflammation within one or more of the sinus chambers in the skull). Bacterial, viral or fungal germs, foreign bodies, growths, tooth abscesses or eye disease can be the cause.

Like humans, dogs possess air-filled spaces in the bones of their skulls (sinuses) which can become diseased. Infections or tumours can occur in these cavities. Sometimes an infection can spread into them from a bad tooth root nearby.

The signs of sinusitis will include sneezing, persistent nasal discharge and head shaking. If you notice these symptoms, take your dog to the vet. The treatment can involve anti-bacterial or anti-fungal drugs, surgical drainage or dental work as appropriate.

Respiratory problems

Dogs can suffer from bronchitis, pleurisy, pneumonia, heart disease and other chest conditions. Coughing and sneezing, the signs of a 'head cold', possibly together with mattery eyes, diarrhoea and listlessness, may indicate distemper – a serious virus disease.

> **COMMON SYMPTOMS**
> • The dog may cough
> • There may be some wheezing and sneezing
> • The dog's breathing may be laboured.

Distemper

Although this is more common in younger animals, it can occur at any age and shows a variety of symptom combinations. Dogs catching distemper can recover although the outlook is serious if there are symptoms such as fits, uncontrollable limb twitching or paralysis, which suggest that the disease has affected the nervous system. These may not appear until many weeks after the virus first invades the body.

What you can do Your dog should be vaccinated against distemper as well as the other important canine viral and leptospiral diseases at the first opportunity – when he is a puppy, usually after six weeks of age. Most vets advise that you keep the annual booster dose going, so ask your vet for advice on this. At the first signs of any generalized illness, perhaps resembling 'flu' or a 'cold', contact the vet. Keep the dog warm, give him plenty of liquids and provide easily digestible nourishing food.

Your vet will be able to confirm

whether your dog has distemper. Because it is caused by a virus, the disease is very difficult to treat. Antibiotics and other drugs are used to suppress any dangerous secondary bacterial infections. Vitamin injections will help to strengthen the body's defences.

Coughs

Where troublesome coughs occur in the older dog, give a half to two codeine tablets three times a day, depending on the animal's size, but see the vet.

Heart disease

This is common in elderly dogs and often responds well to treatment. Under veterinary supervision, drugs can give a new lease of life to dogs with 'dicky' hearts. It is useful in cases of heart trouble and in all older dogs to give vitamin E in the synthetic form (50–200mgm per day depending on the dog's size) or as wheat germ oil capsules (two to six per day).

Bronchitis

Inflammation of the tubes that conduct air through the lungs can be caused by a variety of bacteria and viruses, parasitic lungworms, allergy, inhalation of dust, smoke, foreign bodies or excessive barking. Specific therapy is applied by the vet and sometimes, in the case of foreign bodies, surgery or the use of a fibre-optic bronchoscope is necessary.

Pneumonia

There are many causes of pneumonia in dogs, the commonest being infections by micro-organisms such as viruses or bacteria. Migrating parasitic worm larvae and inhalation of foreign bodies are less frequent. The signs are faster and/or more laboured breathing, a cough, raised temperature and, often, nasal discharge. It can be treated with antibiotics, corticosteroids, 'cough' medicines and medication to relieve symptoms. Pneumonia always demands immediate professional attention.

Kennel cough

This is caused by a bacterium (*Bordetella*) or viruses (Canine parainfluenza virus, Canine herpes virus or Canine adenovirus) or a mixture of these. The signs are a dry cough, often with sneezing, and a moderate eye and nostril discharge. Dogs can be protected by special vaccines administered either by injection or, in some cases, as nasal drops.

Tummy problems

There are numerous causes for tummy troubles in a dog, but if you are worried about your Border Collie or find that the symptoms persist for longer than twelve hours, you should always consult your veterinary surgeon.

If your dog only has a minor tummy upset, you could try feeding him some plain boiled rice or pasta together with white fish, or some other bland meal. Feed this for a couple of days or so until his symptoms improve.

Vomiting

Vomiting may be simple and transient due to either a mild infection (gastritis) of the stomach or to food poisoning. However, if it is severe, persistent or accompanied by other major signs, it can indicate serious conditions, such as distemper, infectious canine hepatitis, an intestinal obstruction, leptospirosis or a heavy worm infestation. In this case, seek veterinary attention urgently.

The usual treatment for vomiting is to replace lost liquids (see diarrhoea below) and give the affected dog one to three teaspoons of Milk of Magnesia, depending on his size, once every three hours.

Diarrhoea

This may be nothing more than the result of a surfeit of liver or a mild bowel infection. However, diarrhoea can be more serious and profuse where important bacteria are present, in certain types of poisoning and in some allergies. Again, you should take your dog to the vet as soon as possible.

For mild cases of diarrhoea in a dog, cut out solid food, milk and fatty things in his diet. Give your dog fluids – best of all are glucose and water or some weak bouillon cube broth – little and often is best. Ice cubes can also be supplied for licking. Keep the animal warm and indoors.

Constipation

If your dog is constipated and is not passing any stools, it may be due to age, a faulty diet including too much chomped-up bone, or to an obstruction. Don't use castor oil on constipated dogs. Give liquid paraffin (a half to two tablespoons). Where an animal is otherwise well but you know he is bunged up with something like bone which, after being crunched up, will set like cement in the bowels, you could get a suitable enema from the chemist.

Flatulence

'Windy' dogs may be the product of a faulty or changed diet. Often flatulence is associated with food that is too low in fibre although, paradoxically, too much fibre can have a similar effect. Generally, adjusting the diet to one of high digestibility and low residue will do the trick. Adding bran to the dog's food will alleviate many cases.

Blood in the stools

This condition can arise from a variety of minor and major causes. It may be from nothing more than a splinter of bone scraping the rectal lining, or the cause may be more serious, such as the dangerous leptospiral infection. Your vet will be able to identify the cause and advise on suitable treatment.

Malabsorption

Some dogs with chronic diarrhoea (often rather fatty looking), associated with a strong appetite but loss of weight, are not able to digest or absorb their food normally. The causes include enzyme deficiency (liver or pancreas faults) or disease of the bowel walls. The vet will employ a variety of tests to establish the cause and prescribe the appropriate therapy. Dogs deficient in pancreatic enzymes can be given pancreatic extract supplements with their food.

Polydipsia and polyphagia

Both of these conditions – polydipsia (drinking more than normal) and polyphagia (eating more than normal) – can be associated with diabetes, disease of the adrenal glands, kidney disease and other conditions. Careful examination of the patient by the vet, together with laboratory tests on blood and/or urine samples, is necessary to pinpoint the cause and thus lead to the correct treatment.

Salmonella infection

Salmonella is a type of bacterium that occurs in a wide variety of strains (serotypes) which may cause disease in, or be carried symptomlessly by, almost any species of animal. Sometimes salmonella can be found in the droppings of apparently normal healthy dogs. Dogs can contract salmonellosis by eating infected food, especially meat and eggs, or by coming into contact with rodents or their droppings, other infected dogs or, more rarely, reptiles or birds. The most common symptoms include diarrhoea (sometimes bloody), vomiting, stomach pain and even collapse, sometimes ending in death.

Diagnosis is confirmed by the vet sending away some samples for bacteriological culture and identification. Treatment is by means of specific antibiotics and fluid replacement. However, it is worth remembering that salmonella infection in animals may be transmissible to humans.

Parvovirus infection

This virus disease is spread via faeces. The incubation period is five to ten days and symptoms vary from sudden death in young pups, through severe vomiting, foul-smelling diarrhoea (often bloody), reduced appetite and depression to bouts of diarrhoea.

Treatment includes replacing lost fluid, anti-vomiting and anti-diarrhoea drugs and antibiotics. Puppies can be vaccinated against parvovirus from eight weeks of age either separately, or, best, in a combination vaccine against all the important canine diseases.

Acute abdomen

The sudden onset of severe pain, vomiting with or without diarrhoea and the collapse of the dog into shock is an emergency that necessitates immediate veterinary attention. The cause may be a powerful, rapidly-developing infection, obstruction of the intestine by a foreign body or a twist of the bowel itself, torsion (twisting) of the stomach, acute kidney, liver or uterine disease or poisoning. Successful treatment depends on quick diagnosis.

Urinary problems

Male dogs will urinate many times a day, in the course of a walk or a run in the garden. Bitches generally urinate less often. The usual signs of urinary disease are increased thirst and urination.

> **COMMON SYMPTOMS**
> • Difficulty in passing urine
> • Urination is frequent
> • Blood is present in the dog's urine
> • More thirsty than usual.

Leptospirosis

This is the most common disease of a dog's kidneys. Humans can be infected by contact with dogs who suffer from this. Symptoms can be acute with loss of appetite, depression, back pain, vomiting, thirst, foul breath and mouth ulcers, or more chronic with loss of weight and frequent urination. It can be diagnosed by blood and urine tests and treated with antibiotics. Vaccination is also available.

Cystitis

This inflammation of the bladder generally responds well to effective treatment with antibiotics, such as ampicillin, perhaps together with medicines that alter the acidity of the urine and urinary sedatives.

Calculi

A diagnosis of stones (calculi) in the urinary system can be confirmed by your vet. In most cases, they are easily removed surgically under general anaesthetic.

Kidney disease

Kidney disease always needs careful management and supervision of diet. Chronic kidney disease patients can live to a ripe old age if the water, protein and mineral content of the diet are regulated, bacterial infection controlled, protein loss minimized and stress of any sort avoided. Prescription diets for chronic kidney cases are available from the veterinary surgeon and good pet shops.

Skeletal problems

The most common skeletal problems in dogs are arthritis and slipped disc. Arthritis is much more common in elderly dogs than in young ones, and it invariably follows hip dysplasia.

Arthritis

This painful condition may arise from the congenital weakness of certain joints,

> **COMMON SYMPTOMS**
> • The dog may be lame
> • He may experience difficulty getting up
> • His gait may be stiff, slow or unusual
> • There may be painful spots on bones or joints.

their over-use/excessive wear, injuries, infections and nutritional faults. Treatment in dogs is similar to that in humans, and your veterinary surgeon may well prescribe corticosteroids, non-steroidal anti-inflammatory drugs and various analgesics.

In some cases, massages, perhaps with anti-inflammatory gels or creams, homoeopathic remedies and acupuncture can also afford some relief as well as improved mobility. However, if you are considering trying out alternative medical treatment on your dog, you should always consult your vet first.

If your dog has arthritis, you should avoid taking him out in very cold or wet weather, and buy him a snug, warm coat to wear for outdoor use. Provide daily multivitamins and minerals and give elderly dogs, in particular, one to four capsules or teaspoons (depending on size) of halibut liver oil.

Painful joints

Arthritis can result in the thickening of the joint capsule, abnormal new bone forming round the joint edges, and wearing of the joint cartilage. The joint is enlarged and painful and its movement is restricted. It tends to affect the shoulders, hips, elbows and stifles.

Obesity

Carrying excess weight can put extra strain on a dog's joints. You can slim down an overweight dog by modifying his diet (reducing carbohydrates and fats), feeding him special canned slimming rations, desisting from giving him sweet titbits, and increasing his exercise gradually. You may find that your veterinary surgery may even run a slimming programme; expert guidance will be provided and your dog's progress monitored by regular weighing.

Slipped disc

The dog's adjacent spinal vertebrae are separated by discs, which are shaped rather like draughts pieces, and act as shock absorbers when functioning correctly. With the passing of time, as dogs grow older, the discs lose their elasticity and become more brittle, less compressible and degenerated. Then, a sudden movement or trauma can cause a disc to 'burst' with the discharge of crunchy material that piles up against the spinal cord or a nerve root with the consequent rapid onset of symptoms. The disc itself does not actually 'slip' out of line with the spine. Border Collies are far less susceptible to 'slipped discs' than breeds with long backs and short legs, such as the Dachshund and Pekingese.

Symptoms and treatment

The signs of a slipped disc include the following: sudden onset of neck or back pain, paralysis or weakness of the limbs, loss of sensation, limb spasms and loss of control of the bladder. Accurate diagnosis is aided by X-rays.

Treatment is by means of medication (analgesics, sedatives, anti-inflammatory drugs and anabolic hormones) and, in some instances, surgery to relieve the pressure on nervous tissues. Good nursing by the owner of the dog under veterinary advice is essential for the animal's recovery.

Skin problems

There are many kinds of skin disease that can affect dogs, and their diagnosis needs examination and often sample analysis by the vet. If you suspect skin problems, seek expert advice.

COMMON SYMPTOMS
- **Thin or bald patches in the coat**
- **Scratching and licking**
- **Wet, dry or crusty sores.**

Healthy tips
- Feed a balanced diet with sufficient fats
- Never apply creams, powders or ointments without trimming back the hair. Let oxygen get to the inflamed area
- Groom your dog regularly to keep his skin and coat healthy.

Mange
This can be caused by an invisible mite and can be seen as crusty, hairless sores. Fleas, lice and ticks can also cause damage to a dog's coat (see page 105). If you see or suspect the presence of any of these skin parasites, you must obtain a specially formulated antiparasitic product from the pet shop, chemist or your vet and treat your dog immediately.

Powders are of little use against mange, and drugs in bath or aerosol form are more appropriate. Tough, deep forms of mange, such as demodectic mange, may be treated by your veterinary surgeon using a combination of baths and drugs given by mouth.

As there are several different types of mange, ask the vet to advise you on the best method of treating your particular case. With all anti-parasite treatment of skin diseases, it is extremely important that you follow the instructions on the label of the preparation being used.

Ringworm
This subtle ailment may need diagnosis by ultra-violet light examination or fungus culture from a hair specimen. Special drugs, which are given by mouth or applied to the skin, are used for ringworm. Care must be taken to see that human contacts do not pick up the disease from the affected dog.

Lumps and bumps
These may be abscesses, cysts or tumours and they may need surgical attention if they persist and grow larger. The earlier a growing lump is attended to, the simpler it is to eradicate, so you must consult your vet by the time it reaches cherry size.

Hot spots
Sudden, sore, wet 'hot spots' that develop in summer or autumn may be caused by an allergy to pollen and other substances. Use scissors to clip the hair over and round the affected area to a level with the skin, and then apply liquid paraffin. You should consult your vet as the dog may need anti-histamine or corticosteroid creams, injections or tablets. Although they look dramatic, hot spots are quickly settled by treatment.

Nursing a sick dog

In all your dog's ailments, mild or serious, you will normally have to be prepared to do something to look after his welfare, usually acting in the capacity of nurse. This will involve learning some essential nursing techniques, such as how to take the animal's temperature and administer tablets and liquid medicines. When you are treating a sick dog always adopt a confident and positive approach. Be prepared and have everything ready in advance. Your dog will be reassured by your calmness.

Taking a temperature

You cannot rely on the state of a dog's nose as an effective indicator of his temperature, good health or sickness. As with children, being able to take your pet's temperature with a thermometer can help you to decide whether or not to call the vet and can also assist him in diagnosing and treating what is wrong.

You should use an ordinary glass thermometer, which you can purchase at most pharmacies. For preference, it should have a stubby rather than a slim bulb, or, better still, you can invest in an unbreakable thermometer, although these are more expensive. Lubricate the thermometer with a little olive oil or petroleum jelly and insert it about 2.5cm (1in) into the dog's rectum.

Once it is in place, you can hold the thermometer with the bulb angled against the rectal wall for good contact. After half a minute, remove and read the thermometer.

Normal temperature range

A dog's normal temperature will be in the range of 38–38.6°C (101–101.6°F). Taking into account a slight rise for nervousness or excitement in some dogs, you can expect under such conditions to read up to 38.7°C (101.8°F) or even 38.8°C (102°F). Higher than that is abnormal. Always shake down the mercury in the thermometer before use, and be sure to clean and disinfect the instrument afterwards.

Administering medicine

Try to avoid putting medicines into your dog's food or drink, as this can be a very imprecise method. However, for dogs that are really averse to pills and capsules, you can conceal them in tasty titbits, but you must check that the dog has swallowed them.

Tablets, pills or capsules

Tablets, pills or capsules should always be dropped into the 'V'-shaped groove at the back of the dog's mouth while holding it open, with one thumb pressed firmly against the hard roof of the dog's mouth. Then close the mouth again and gently massage the dog's throat to encourage swallowing.

Liquids

These should be given slowly to a dog, a little at a time, by the same method or direct into the lip pouch with the dog's mouth closed. They can also be squirted through a syringe.

Handling your dog

It is very useful to know how to handle and restrain your dog effectively during visits to the vet, especially if he gets anxious about being examined or may even behave aggressively.

Making a makeshift muzzle

A muzzle is essential when a nervous, possessive, aggressive or sensitive dog is in pain and has to be handled or examined. To make one, you can use a length of bandage, string, nylon stocking or even a tie – it will prevent the owner and vet being bitten.

By carefully positioning the muzzle not too far back, you can still administer liquid medicine by pouring it into the gap between the dog's lips behind the encircling band.

1 Tie a knot in the bandage and wrap it around the dog's muzzle.
2 Cross the ends of the bandage at the bottom under the jaw.
3 Bring the ends round to the back of the dog's head and tie firmly.

At the vet's

It is important to know how to handle your dog when you visit the vet's surgery. Although some dogs trot in happily and do not mind being examined, others can be nervous and may even panic. Very large dogs are usually looked at on the floor, but the vet will want to examine small to medium-sized dogs on the examination table and you will have to lift your dog up if so.

Lifting your dog

To avoid injury, not only to your dog but also to your back, always bend your knees when picking him up. Support his body properly with one hand on his chest between the front legs and the other below his rear.

1 If lifting a medium-sized dog, bend your knees and place one hand securely under his rear and the other around his chest.
2 With your hand at the rear, taking most of the dog's weight and holding him securely, rise onto one knee, keeping your back straight.
3 Keep the dog in a secure position, holding him close to your body, then rise to your feet, bringing him up to chest height.

First aid

First aid is the emergency care given to a dog suffering injury or illness of sudden onset. The aims of first aid are to keep the dog alive, avoid unnecessary suffering and prevent further injury.

Rules of first aid

- Always keep calm: if you panic, you will be unable to help the dog
- Contact a vet as soon as possible: advice given over the phone may be life-saving.
- Avoid any injury to yourself: a distressed or injured dog may bite, so use a muzzle if necessary
- Control any haemorrhage: excessive blood loss can lead to severe shock and even death
- Maintain an airway: failure to breathe or obtain adequate oxygen can lead to brain damage or loss of life.

Accidents and emergencies

Common accidents and emergencies require you to have a basic knowledge of first aid. In emergencies, your priorities are to keep your dog comfortable until he can be examined by a vet. However, in many cases, there is important action you can do immediately to help preserve your dog's health and life.

Burns

These can be caused by very hot liquids or by contact with an electrical current or various types of caustic, acid or irritant liquid. You must act quickly.

Electrical burns

Most electrical burns are the result of a dog chewing a live flex or cable, so wires should always be hidden, particularly from puppies, and electrical devices unplugged after use. Biting live wires can cause burns to the inside of the lips and the gums but may, in the worst cases, result in shock, collapse and death.

Recommended action First, switch off the electricity before you handle the patient. Examine the insides of the mouth and apply cold water to any burnt areas. If the gums are whiter than normal or blue-tinged, shock may be present. You must seek veterinary advice.

Chemical burns

Burns can also be caused by caustic chemicals, and you must seek veterinary attention if this happens.

Recommended action Wash the affected area with copious warm soapy water and then seek veterinary advice.

Scalding with a liquid

Hot water or oil spillage commonly occurs in the kitchen. Although the dog's coat affords him some insulating protection, the skin beneath may well be damaged with visible signs only emerging after several hours have passed in many cases.

Recommended action You must apply plenty of cold water immediately to the affected area and follow this by holding an ice pack on the burn – a bag of frozen peas is ideal. Then gently dry the burnt zone with mineral oil (liquid paraffin) and seek veterinary advice.

Poisoning

The house, the garden and the world outside contain a multitude of substances, both natural and artificial, that can poison a dog. If you suspect that your dog has been poisoned, you must contact your vet right away. Frequently some symptoms, such as vomiting, blood in the dog's stools or collapse, which owners may imagine to be the result of poisoning, are actually caused by other kinds of illness.

A dog may come into contact with various poisonous chemicals through ingestion or by licking his coat when it is contaminated by a noxious substance. Canine inquisitiveness and the tendency to scavenge can lead some dogs to eat or drink some strange materials. Sometimes owners will negligently give dangerous substances to their pets. Occasionally, poisonous gases or vapours are inhaled by animals.

Types of poison

All our homes contain highly poisonous compounds, including weedkillers, pesticides (rat, slug and insect killers), fungicides, disinfectants, car antifreeze, lead compounds, caustic cleaning fluids, paint thinners, creosote and excessive amounts of patent medicines, such as paracetamol and aspirin.

Common poisons

- Mouse and rat killer
- Sleeping tablets
- Carbon monoxide gas in faulty heaters and car exhausts
- Weedkillers
- Corrosive chemicals, such as acids, alkalis, bleach, carbolic acid, phenols, creosote and petroleum products
- Antifreeze
- Lead paint, solders, putty and fishing weights
- Slug pellets
- Insecticides
- Rodenticides (warfarin)
- Herbicides
- Illegal bird baits.

Poisoning can also be caused outside in the garden, park or countryside by certain plants, insect stings and the venom of snakes and toads.

Poisonous plants

Many owners do not realize that their gardens contain dangerous plants. These include the bulbs of many spring flowers, holly and mistletoe berries, the leaves and flowers of rhododendrons and hydrangeas, leaves of yew, box and laurels, sweetpea, wisteria and bluebell seeds, and all parts of the columbine, hemlock, lily of the valley and ivy. Some fungi are as poisonous to dogs as they are to humans, as are the blue-green algae that sometimes bloom on garden ponds in hot weather. Keep your dog away from these plants.

Recommended action Determining
which poison is involved can be quite
difficult if you don't know what the
dog has come into contact with. Early
professional diagnosis is vital.

1 Look for any evidence of burning
or blistering in the dog's mouth caused
by corrosive poisons.

2 Flush out the mouth with warm water
and let him drink water or milk.

Corrosive substances

1 Wipe clean the contaminated area
with rags or paper tissues and cut off
congealed masses of hair with scissors.
Cooking oil or petroleum jelly will help
soften paint and tar.

2 Wash thoroughly with dog or baby
shampoo and rinse well. Don't use paint
thinners, concentrated washing
detergents, solvents or turpentine.

If the poison has been swallowed
recently (within one hour), try to make
the dog vomit by giving him either a
hazelnut-sized chunk of washing soda
(sodium carbonate) or some English
mustard powder (a level teaspoon in half
a cup of water for a medium-sized dog,
and pro rata).

Bee and wasp stings

Painful, but usually single and with
no serious general effects, insect stings
require little more than removal of the
sting itself in the case of bee stings (wasps
and hornets do not leave their stings
behind) by means of tweezers and the
application of antihistamine cream.
Rarely, death can ensue if a dog is subject
to a large number, perhaps hundreds, of
stings. Stings can also be serious if the
tongue or mouth are involved.

Recommended action If your dog
goes into shock, he will need anti-shock
therapy, such as intravenous fluids,
adrenalin and antihistamine injections.
Keep him warm and make sure that his
breathing is unimpeded while you obtain
veterinary attention.

Snake bites

Britain's only venomous snake, the
common adder, may sometimes bite
a dog who disturbs it.

Recommended action You must take the dog straight to the vet for treatment with adder anti-venom – do not delay.

Bleeding

The appearance of blood anywhere on a dog's body will always necessitate immediate close inspection. A variety of accidents and some diseases may produce blood from the nostrils, eyes or ears or in the droppings or in vomited material. None of the above types of haemorrhage are usually suitable for first aid by the owner. All need veterinary attention, however, though the causes may often be trivial and ephemeral.

Bleeding from the body surface through wounds inflicted during fights, traffic accidents or other traumatic incidents can be copious, and this does require prompt first aid.

Recommended action The most important thing you can do is to apply pressure to the wound. Hand or finger pressure is always invaluable until a pad of gauze or cotton wool can be found. This should be soaked in cold water, placed on the wound and kept in place by constant firm pressure or, better still, a bandage. Take the dog to a veterinary surgery as quickly as possible. Do not waste any time applying antiseptic ointments or powders to a significantly bleeding wound.

Heat stroke

Every summer we read in the newspapers of cases of dogs dying from heat stroke as a result of the gross thoughtlessness and negligence of their owners.

Just like babies and young children, dogs who are left in hot and poorly ventilated spaces, particularly parked cars, and sometimes without water, will overheat.

COMMON SYMPTOMS
- **Inability to control internal body temperature**
- **As the latter rises, the dog will become distressed, pant rapidly and will quickly weaken**
- **The dog's mouth will appear much redder than normal**
- **Collapse, coma and even death can follow in a reasonably short space of time, so you must act quickly.**

Recommended action Cooling the affected dog's body, particularly his head, by means of cold water baths, hosing down with cold water and ice packs is essential. If the temperature-regulating mechanism in the brain has already been seriously damaged a fatal outcome may still ensue. Veterinary attention must be obtained immediately. Of course, however, by being a responsible and thoughtful owner, you can prevent such emergencies occurring.

Foreign bodies

These can occur in various parts of a dog's anatomy and the treatment will vary according to the type of foreign body and its location.

In the eye

Foreign bodies in the eye will cause the dog to rub his head on the ground and paw at his eye.

Recommended action Flood the affected eye with human-type eye drops or olive oil to float out the foreign body. Do not use tweezers close to the eyeball.

In the ear
Both plant seeds and grass awns are particularly likely to get into a dog's ears during summer walks. Their presence will cause itching and irritation. The affected dog will shake his head and scratch and paw at his ears.

Recommended action Pour some warm olive oil or other vegetable oil into the dog's ear, filling it. The object may float to the surface and can then be picked up by tweezers. Deeper, embedded foreign bodies will always require veterinary attention.

In the mouth
Pieces of bone or splinters of wood can become lodged in a dog's mouth. The offending object may be jammed between the left and right upper molars at the back of the mouth or between two adjacent teeth. Less commonly, an object, such as a small ball, gets stuck in a dog's throat. In all cases, he will show symptoms of distress, including pawing at the mouth, gagging, trying to retch or shaking his head.

Recommended action While someone holds the dog firmly, you should open his mouth and try to dislodge the foreign body with a spoon or kitchen tongs. Where the dog is having difficulty breathing and literally choking, try holding him upside down, massaging the throat and slapping his back. If you cannot remove the object, you must seek veterinary help at once.

In the paws
Splinters of glass, thorns, particles of metal and even fragments of stone can penetrate the pads on a dog's paws or lodge in the skin between the toes. As a result, the dog limps and usually licks the affected paw.

Recommended action If the object is visible, you can remove it with tweezers. However, if it cannot be seen, because of being embedded, then bathe the foot two to three times daily in warm water and salt (a teaspoon of salt to a cupful of water) until the foreign body emerges from the softened skin. If lameness persists for more than a day or two, you must seek veterinary attention as infection may set in.

Fish hooks
You must never attempt to pull out a fish hook, wherever it is. Instead, use pliers to cut the end of the fish hook and then push the barbed end out through the skin. If it looks sore, then rub in some antiseptic cream.

Useful information

Organizations

Association of Pet Behaviour Counsellors
PO Box 46, Worcester WR8 9YS
tel: 01386 751151
www.apbc.org.ok

The Association of Pet Dog Trainers
P.O. Box 17, Kempsford,
Gloucester GL7 4W2
tel: 01285 810811
www.apdt.co.uk

British Veterinary Association
7 Mansfield Street, London W1M 0AT
tel: 020 7636 6541
www.bva.co.uk

DEFRA
Ergon House, c/o Nobel House
17 Smith Square, London SW1P 3JR
tel: 020 7238 6951
www.defra.gov.uk

International Sheep Dog Society
Clifton House, 4a Goldington Road,
Bedford MK40 3NF
tel: 01234 352672
www.isds.org.uk

The Kennel Club
1–5 Clarges Street, Piccadilly,
London W1Y 8AB
tel: 0870 606 6750
www.thekennelclub.org.uk

Rescue organizations:

Border Collie Trust of Great Britain
Heath Way, Narrow Lane,
Colton, nr. Rugeley,
Staffs WS15 3LY
tel: 01889 577058
www.bordercollietrustgb.org.uk

RSPCA
Causeway, Horsham,
W. Sussex RH12 1HG
tel: 01403 264181
www.RSPCA.org.uk

Blue Cross
Shilton Road, Burford,
Oxford OX18 4PF
tel: 01993 822651
www.bluecross.org.uk

Magazines

Dog World
www.dogworld.co.uk

Dogs Monthly
www.dogsmonthly.co.uk

Dogs Today
www.dogstodaymagazine.co.uk

Our Dogs
www.ourdogs.co.uk

Your Dog
www.yourdog.co.uk

Websites

Border Collie Club of Great Britain
www.bordercollieclub.com

Dogs Trust
www.dogstrust.org.uk

National Dog Tattoo Register
www.dog-register.co.uk

Obedience website
www.ObedienceUK.com

Petlog
www.thekennelclub.org.uk/meet/petlog.
html

UK Registry of Canine Behaviourists
www.ukrcb.org

Index